STERLING
Test Prep

LAW ESSENTIALS

Civil Procedure

Governing Law

3rd edition

Copyright © 2022 Sterling Test Prep

All rights reserved. This publication's content, including the text and graphic images or part thereof, may not be reproduced, downloaded, disseminated, published, converted to electronic media, or distributed by any means whatsoever without prior written consent from the publisher. Copyright infringement violates federal law and is subject to criminal and civil penalties.

This publication is designed to provide accurate and authoritative information regarding the subject matter covered. It is distributed with the understanding that the publisher, authors, or editors are not engaged in rendering legal or another professional service. If legal advice or other expert assistance is required, a competent professional's services should be sought.

Sterling Test Prep is not legally liable for mistakes, omissions, or inaccuracies in this publication's content. Sterling Test Prep does not guarantee that the user of this publication will pass the bar exam or achieve a performance level. Individual performance depends on many factors, including but not limited to the level of preparation, aptitude, and individual performance on test day.

3 2 1

ISBN-13: 978-1-9547252-1-8

Sterling Test Prep products are available at quantity discounts.

For more information, contact info@sterling–prep.com.

Sterling Test Prep
6 Liberty Square #11
Boston, MA 02109

©2022 Sterling Test Prep

Published by Sterling Test Prep

Printed in the U.S.A.

Customer Satisfaction Guarantee

Your feedback is important because we strive to provide the highest quality prep materials. Email us comments or suggestions.

info@sterling–prep.com

We reply to emails – check your spam folder

Thank you for choosing our book!

STERLING
Test Prep

Thousands of students use our study aids to prepare for law school exams and to pass the bar!

Passing the bar is essential for admission to practice law and launching your legal career.

This preparation guide describes the principles of substantive law governing the correct answers to exam questions. It was developed by legal professionals and law instructors who possess extensive credentials and have been admitted to practice law in several jurisdictions. The content is clearly presented and systematically organized for targeted preparation.

The performance on individual questions has been correlated with success or failure on the bar. By analyzing previously administered exams, the authors identified these predictive items and assembled the rules of law that govern the answers to questions tested. Learn the essential governing law to make fine-line distinctions among related principles and decide between tough choices on the exam. This knowledge is vital to excel in law school finals and pass the bar exam.

We look forward to being an essential part of your preparation and wish you great success in the legal profession!

Law Essentials series

Constitutional Law

Contracts

Evidence

Real Property

Torts

Civil Procedure

Criminal Law and Criminal Procedure

Business Associations

Conflict of Laws

Family Law

Secured Transactions

Trusts and Estates

Visit our Amazon store

Comprehensive Glossary of Legal Terms

Over 2,100 essential legal terms defined and explained. An excellent reference source for law students, practitioners and readers seeking an understanding of legal vocabulary and its application.

Landmark U.S. Supreme Court Cases: Essential Summaries

Learn important constitutional cases that shaped American law. Understand how the evolving needs of society intersect with the U.S. Constitution. Short summaries of seminal Supreme Court cases focused on issues and holdings.

Visit our Amazon store

Table of Contents

CIVIL PROCEDURE GOVERNING LAW (Federal Rules of Civil Procedure) ... 15

Federal Jurisdiction ... 17
Original and appellate jurisdiction of the Supreme Court ... 17
Cases and controversies ... 17
Article III – Judicial Branch ... 17

Jurisdiction of Federal Courts ... 21
Subject matter jurisdiction ... 21

Federal Question Jurisdiction ... 23
The meaning of "arising under" ... 23
Federal question must appear in the complaint ... 23
Concurrent and exclusive federal jurisdiction ... 23

Diversity Jurisdiction ... 25
The requirement of complete diversity ... 25
Citizenship ... 25
Realignment or substitution of parties ... 26
Amount-in-controversy requirement ... 26
Aggregation of claims ... 27
Jurisdictional amount in counterclaims ... 27
Structure of the United States court systems (*flowchart*) ... 28

Supplemental Jurisdiction ... 29
Supplemental jurisdiction rules ... 29
Exceptions to supplemental jurisdiction ... 29

Removal Jurisdiction ... 31
Prerequisites to removal – federal subject matter ... 31
Only the defendant can remove ... 31
Separate and independent claim ... 31
Procedure for removal ... 31
Remand ... 32

Jurisdiction Over Persons and Property ... 33
Statutory limits of jurisdiction ... 33
Relationship between defendant and forum state ... 33

Service of Process and Notice ... 35
Summons and complaint ... 35
Adequate notice ... 35
Personal and corporate service ... 35

CIVIL PROCEDURE GOVERNING LAW (continued)

Venue, *Forum Non Conveniens* and Transfer 37
    Purpose and waiver 37
    Venue rules 37
    Residence for venue purposes 37
    Transfer – improper venue 38
    Venue is proper for convenience 38
    Forum non conveniens 38

Law Applied by Federal Courts 39
    Vertical choice of law 39
    Horizontal choice of law 39

Pretrial Procedures 41
    Preliminary injunctions and temporary restraining orders 41
    Interlocutory injunctions 41
    Pleadings 41
    Counterclaims and crossclaims 43
    Amended and supplemental pleadings 43

Rule 11 – Ethical Restraints in Pleadings 45
    Veracity of pleadings 45
    Nonfrivolous claims 45
    Sanctions for violations 45

Pretrial Motions 47
    Rule 12 pre-answer motions 47
    Amending the complaint 47

Joinder 49
    Rule 8 joinder 49
    Counterclaims 49
    Crossclaims 49
    Joinder of parties 49

Discovery 51
    Automatic disclosure 51
    Common objections of discovery 52
    Discovery sanctions 52
    Depositions 53
    Interrogatories 53
    Production of documents 54
    Physical and mental exams 54
    Request for admissions 54

CIVIL PROCEDURE GOVERNING LAW (continued)

Adjudication Without a Trial 55
- Voluntary dismissal 55
- Involuntary dismissal 55
- Dismissing counterclaims, crossclaim or third-party claims 56

Pretrial Conference and Order 57
- Pretrial conferences 57

Jury Trials 59
- Right to a jury trial – demand 59
- Selection and composition of juries 59
- Number of jurors, verdict and polling 59
- Jury instructions 60
- Instructions to the jury for objections 61
- Instructions to the jury preserving a claim of error 61

Motions 63
- Pretrial motions 63
- Summary judgment 63
- Declaratory judgment 64
- Directed verdict – judgment as a matter of law (JMOL) 64
- Summary judgment versus directed verdict 65
- Seventh Amendment considerations 65
- Standards of review 66
- Judgment notwithstanding verdict (JNOV) 67
- Motions for a new trial 68
- Granting the renewed motion 69
- Conditional ruling on a motion for a new trial 69

Verdicts and Judgments 71
- Findings and conclusions by the court 71
- Amended or additional findings 71
- Judgment on partial findings 71
- Entering judgment 72
- Relief from a judgment or order 73
- Claim preclusion – *res judicata* 74
- Issue preclusion – collateral estoppel 77

Appeals and Review with Government as a Party 79
- Appeal as of right 79

CIVIL PROCEDURE GOVERNING LAW (*continued*)

Appeals and Review for Civil Cases ... 81
- Effect of a motion on a notice of appeal ... 81
- Motion for extension of time ... 81
- Reopening the time to file an appeal ... 82
- Entry defined ... 82

Appeals and Review for Criminal Cases ... 83
- Effect of a motion on a notice of appeal ... 83
- Motion for extension of time ... 84
- Appeal by an inmate confined in an institution ... 84
- Mistaken filing in the court of appeals ... 85

Civil procedure – Quick Facts ... 87
- American courts: basic principles ... 87
- Diversity jurisdiction ... 88
- Arising-under jurisdiction ... 88
- Removal to federal court ... 89
- The evolution of personal jurisdiction ... 90
- Long-arm statutes ... 91
- Basic venue ... 91

Review Questions ... 95
- Multiple-choice questions ... 95
- True/false questions ... 100
- Answer keys ... 104

EXAM INFORMATION, PREPARATION AND TEST-TAKING STRATEGIES ... 105

Introduction to the Uniform Bar Examination (UBE) ... 107
- Structure of the UBE ... 107
- The Multistate Bar Examination (MBE) ... 107
- Interpreting the UBE score report ... 107
- The importance of the MBE score ... 108
- MEE and MPT scores ... 109
- The objective of the Multistate Bar Exam ... 109

Preparation Strategies for the Bar Exam ... 111
- An effective bar exam study schedule and plan ... 111
- Focused studying ... 112
- Advice on using outlines ... 112
- Easy questions make the difference ... 113

EXAM INFORMATION, PREP & TEST-TAKING STRATEGIES (continued)

Preparation Strategies for the Bar Exam (continued)
- Study plan based upon statistics 114
- Factors associated with passing the bar 114
- Pass rates based on GPA and LSAT scores 115

Learning and Applying the Substantive Law 117
- Knowledge of substantive law 117
- Where to find the law 118
- Controlling authority 118
- Recent changes in the law 119
- Lesser-known issues and unusual applications 119
- Practice applying the governing law 119
- Know which governing law is being tested 120
- Answers which are always wrong 120

Honing Reading Skills 121
- Understanding complex transactions 121
- Impediments to careful reading 121
- Reading too much into a question 121
- Read the call of the question first 122
- Negative calls 122
- Read all choices 122
- Broad statements of black letter law may be correct 122

Multiple-Choice Test-Taking Tactics 123
- Determine the single correct answer 123
- Process of elimination 123
- Elimination increases the odds 123
- Eliminating two wrong answers 124
- Pick the winning side 124
- Distance between choices on the other side 124
- Questions based upon a common fact pattern 125
- Multiple true/false issues 125
- Correctly stated, but the inapplicable principle of law 125
- "Because" questions 126
- "If" questions 126
- "Because" or "if" need not be exclusive 126
- Exam tip for "because" 126
- "Only if" requires exclusivity 127
- "Unless" questions 127
- Limiting words 127

EXAM INFORMATION, PREP & TEST-TAKING STRATEGIES (*continued*)

Making Correct Judgment Calls 129
- Applying the law to the facts 129
- Bad judgment equals the wrong answer 129
- Judgment calls happen 129
- The importance of procedure 130

Exam Tips and Suggestions 131
- Timing is everything 131
- An approach for when time is not an issue 131
- An approach for when time is an issue 132
- Difficult questions 132
- Minimize fatigue to maximize your score 132
- Proofread the answer sheet 133
- Intelligent preparation over a sustained period 133

Essay Preparation Strategies and Essay-Writing Suggestions 135
- Memorize the law 135
- Focus on the highly tested essay rules 135
- Practice writing essay answers each week 135
- Add one essay-specific subject each week 135
- Make it easy for the grader to award points 136
- Conclusion for each essay question 136
- Tips for an easy-to-read essay 137
- Think before you write 137
- The ability to think and communicate like a lawyer 137
- Do not restate the facts 138
- Do not state abstract or irrelevant propositions of law 138
- Discuss all the issues raised 139
- Methods for finding all issues 139
- Indicators requiring alternative arguments 139
- Avoid ambiguous, rambling statements and verbosity 140
- Avoid undue repetition 140
- Avoid slang and colloquialism 140
- Write legibly and coherently 140
- Timing strategies 141
- Stay focused 141
- Law school essay grading matrix 141

APPENDIX 143

Overview of American Law (*diagram*) 145

U.S. Court Systems – Federal and State Courts 147
    Jurisdiction of federal and state courts 147
    Organization of the federal courts 149

How Civil Cases Move Through the Federal Courts 151
    Jury trials 151
    Bench trials 152
    Jury selection 152
    Instructions and standard of proof 152
    Judgment 153
    Right to appeal 153

How Criminal Cases Move Through the Federal Courts 155
    Indictment or information 155
    Arraignment 156
    Investigation 156
    Deliberation and verdict 156
    Judgment and sentencing 157
    Right to appeal 157

How Civil and Criminal Appeals Move Through the Federal Courts 159
    Assignment of judges 159
    Review of a lower court decision 159
    Oral argument 159
    Decision 159
    The Supreme Court of the United States 160

Standards of Review for Federal Courts (*table*) 162

The Constitution of the United States (*a transcription*) 163
    Preamble 163
    Article I 163
    Article II 168
    Article III 170
    Article IV 171
    Article V 171
    Article VI 172
    Article VII 172

APPENDIX (*continued*)

Enactment of the Bill of Rights of the United States of America (1791) 173

The Bill of Rights: Amendments I–X 175

Constitutional Amendments XI–XXVII 177
- Amendment XI 177
- Amendment XII 177
- Amendment XIII 178
- Amendment XIV 178
- Amendment XV 179
- Amendment XVI 179
- Amendment XVII 179
- Amendment XVIII 180
- Amendment XIX 180
- Amendment XX 180
- Amendment XXI 181
- Amendment XXII 182
- Amendment XXIII 182
- Amendment XXIV 182
- Amendment XXV 183
- Amendment XXVI 184
- Amendment XXII 184

States' Rights Under the U.S. Constitution 185
- Selective incorporation under the 14th Amendment 185
- Federalism in the United States 185

Civil Procedure Governing Law

(Federal Rules of Civil Procedure)

The NCBE often tests the same Civil Procedure issues, so master these topics to maximize your test score. Focus on subject matter jurisdiction (diversity jurisdiction, federal question, supplemental jurisdiction), personal jurisdiction, venue, service of process, discovery, pretrial procedures, motions. Other issues tested include jury trials, verdicts and judgments, appeals, and review. Approximately two-thirds of the Civil Procedure questions cover jurisdiction and venue, pretrial procedures, and motions.

The statements herein were compiled by analyzing released Civil Procedure questions and setting forth the principles of law governing the correct answers. Review these principles before preparing answers to practice Civil Procedure questions. Memorize this governing law and understand how it applies to the correct answer.

Per the National Conference of Bar Examiners, assume the application of 1) the Federal Rules of Civil Procedure as currently in effect and 2) sections of Title 28 of the U.S. Code pertaining to trial and appellate jurisdiction, venue, and transfer.

Federal Jurisdiction

Original and appellate jurisdiction of the Supreme Court

Article III, Section 2 of the Constitution provides that:

> "*In all cases affecting ambassadors, other public ministers and consuls, and those in which a state shall be a party, the Supreme Court shall have original jurisdiction.*"

Within the judicial power of the United States,

> "*the Supreme Court shall have appellate jurisdiction, both as to law and fact, with such exceptions, and under such regulations as the Congress shall make.*"

Cases and controversies

The judicial power extends to "*cases*" and "*controversies*."

Factors considered in determining when a case or controversy exists include mootness, standing, ripeness, whether the case involves a political or administrative question, whether a case is collusive or whether the parties are seeking a merely advisory opinion.

Article III – Judicial Branch

Article III of the U.S. Constitution establishes the federal government's judicial branch.

Under Article III, the judicial branch consists of *The* Supreme Court of the United States and lower courts created by Congress.

Article III defines judicial power as resolving "*cases and controversies.*"

Article III prohibits advisory opinions.

The Constitution does not articulate the power of the judicial courts.

The judicial review authority was established in *Marbury v. Madison* (1803), where the court created the authority for federal judicial review of legislative and executive actions.

Marbury declared "*that it's the province of the judicial department to say what the law is.*"

The court sets limits on federal judicial power.

Whether the plaintiff is the proper party to bring a matter to the court for adjudication (i.e., justiciability doctrine) has four requirements:

> standing,
>
> ripeness,
>
> political question, and
>
> mootness.

These doctrines render a controversy "*nonjusticiable*" if a court decides that any of the four essential elements are absent.

1) Standing: a party's ability to demonstrate to the court sufficient connection and harm from the action challenged to support that party's participation in the case.

    The plaintiff must allege and prove actual or imminent injury.

    The plaintiff may assert only personally suffered injuries:

    Sierra Club v. Morton (1971): Disney wanted to build a ski resort. The Sierra Club sued to stop construction, and the Supreme Court ruled the Sierra Club lacked standing.

2) Causation and redressability: the plaintiff must allege and prove that the defendant caused the injury so that a favorable court decision is likely to remedy the injury.

3) No third party standing: a plaintiff cannot represent the claims of others not before the court (i.e., must be a personal injury).

    There is an important exception where third-party standing is allowed.

    A plaintiff who meets the other standing requirements and one of the following exceptions may bring a suit with proper standing.

    > A close relationship between the plaintiff and the injured third party.
    >
    > Plaintiff represents the third party adequately.
    >
    > Doctor–patient relationship: laws limiting abortion that inflicted injuries on the doctors (e.g., loss of business), so doctors chose to represent the patient's rights.

    The Supreme Court ruled that a father lacked standing to represent his daughter for the "under God" in school because he did not have legal custody, and the mother did not want the suit to proceed.

    Third-party standing is allowed if the injured party is unlikely to assert their rights (the party cannot appear in court); the plaintiff who meets the other requirements may represent the claims of the aggrieved.

4) No generalized grievances.

   A cause of action is not a generalized grievance because many people (or everyone) are affected by the injury.

   The plaintiff must not be suing solely as a citizen or taxpayer.

   The plaintiff sues as a citizen (or general taxpayer) → generalized grievance → no standing.

   Exception: taxpayers may challenge government expenditures according to a federal statute as violating the *establishment clause*.

   The Supreme Court has held that the establishment clause was a limit on Congressional spending power.

   There is a narrow exception to no generalized grievances. The Supreme Court has held that taxpayers do not have standing for government expenditures of property (money) to religious institutions under a specific federal statute.

   Flast v. Cohn (1968): federal government adopted a statute that provided textbooks, instructional and library materials for religious and sectarian schools.

   Flast had standing. The majority opinion by Chief Justice Earl Warren established a "*double nexus*" test for taxpayer standing.

   (a) Plaintiff must "*establish a logical link*" between status (e.g., taxpayer) and the legislative enactment being challenged,

   (b) Plaintiff must show that the challenged enactment exceeds specific constitutional limitations upon the exercise of the taxing and spending power and *not* merely beyond the powers delegated to Congress by Article I, Section 8.

   Only when both nexuses have been satisfied may the petitioner have the standing to sue.

Notes for active learning

Jurisdiction of Federal Courts

Subject matter jurisdiction

The Constitution limits the subject matter jurisdiction of the federal courts to:

1) suits involving a federal question (e.g., Constitution, federal statutes),

2) suits between citizens of different states for *over* $75,000 (diversity jurisdiction),

3) cases involving ambassadors,

4) admiralty and maritime jurisdiction, and

5) cases where the United States is a party.

Congress has implemented the constitutional provision by imposing additional restrictions on the jurisdiction which federal courts are permitted to exercise, such as the amount-in-controversy requirement.

Subject matter jurisdiction may not be conferred by agreement or consent of the litigants.

The defense of lack of subject matter jurisdiction may be raised at any point in the trial and may be first raised on appeal.

Notes for active learning

Federal Question Jurisdiction

The meaning of "arising under"

A right or immunity created by the Constitution or federal law must be an essential element of the plaintiff's cause of action for the federal district court to have "arising under" jurisdiction.

The fact that the defendant can raise federal law as an affirmative defense in their answer does not confer federal jurisdiction.

Federal question must appear in the complaint

The federal question or constitutional issue must be properly pleaded in the complaint.

The anticipation of a defense based on federal law is insufficient for federal question jurisdiction by the court.

Concurrent and exclusive federal jurisdiction

Absent congressional intent to confer exclusive jurisdiction on the federal courts, both federal and state courts have jurisdiction to try claims based upon federal law.

Congress has granted the federal courts exclusive jurisdiction in:

> bankruptcy proceedings,
>
> patent,
>
> copyright cases,
>
> actions against foreign consuls,
>
> admiralty and maritime cases,
>
> antitrust cases,
>
> cases under the Securities Exchange Act of 1934, and
>
> actions where the United States is a party.

Notes for active learning

Diversity Jurisdiction

The requirement of complete diversity

Congress has not conferred on the federal district courts the jurisdiction of cases between citizens of different states that the Constitution allows it to confer.

The lawsuit must have complete diversity between the parties on each side of the controversy for the court to have jurisdiction. Each plaintiff must be from a state different from each defendant, or one must be a citizen of a state and the other an alien.

The exception is an action for *statutory interpleader*, where parties on each side of the controversy can be citizens of the same state if two states are represented among the parties.

For determining whether the statutory requirements for jurisdiction are met, diversity is determined as of the date the action is commenced; diversity need not have existed when the cause of action arose.

If the defendant impleads a third party whose citizenship is the same as the plaintiff, diversity is not destroyed.

However, while a defendant may be brought in by a third-party complaint by a party with the same citizenship as the plaintiff, the plaintiff may not amend the complaint to add such a person as a party defendant.

Citizenship

Citizenship of a natural person for purposes of determining diversity means the state of that party's domicile.

A person's original domicile is the domicile of their parents.

When reaching adulthood, a person can change domicile by being physically present in a place they select as their fixed residence.

Domicile can subsequently be changed by physical presence in the new domicile with the intent to remain there indefinitely.

The citizenship of a corporation for diversity purposes is:

    1) the state of incorporation and

    2) the state in which it has its principal place of business.

A partnership, labor union, or other unincorporated association as a party has each member's citizenship determine diversity.

If a deceased person's estate is a party, the decedent's citizenship controls for diversity.

The citizenship of the executor or administrator is irrelevant.

In an action on behalf of a trust, the trustee's citizenship (not beneficiary's) controls.

For diversity purposes in class actions, the named representatives' citizenship controls.

Realignment or substitution of parties

Diversity may be created or destroyed by a realignment of the parties according to their interest in the dispute.

If a party is named a plaintiff and is a defendant, they are classified as a defendant when determining if complete diversity exists.

The initial party's citizenship governs the substitution of parties because of death, incompetence, or public office succession.

Amount-in-controversy requirement

The plaintiff's complaint determines the amount in controversy.

For a federal court to have jurisdiction in a diversity suit, the amount in controversy, as measured by the damages the plaintiff sought in good faith when the suit commenced, must be greater than $75,000.

Recovering less than $75,000.01 does not retroactively destroy jurisdiction.

The dollar value for the amount in controversy requirement of injunctive relief is the value of the right protected or injury to be prevented.

Aggregation of claims

A single plaintiff suing a single defendant may aggregate claims to achieve the jurisdictional amount.

Thus, a claim for personal injury and property damage could be added to exceed $75,000.

If a single plaintiff has claims against several defendants, claims can be aggregate only if the defendants are jointly liable.

Thus, if defendant A and defendant B were joint tortfeasors and the plaintiff's total claim was more than $75,000 against each, the right of contribution might reduce the total amount paid by a tortfeasor to less than $75,000.01 is not relevant for jurisdiction purposes.

Several plaintiffs' claims against a single defendant cannot be aggregated except where several plaintiffs have an undivided right, title, or interest in the claim.

Each member's claims in a class action cannot be aggregated, making it less likely that class action cases based upon state causes of action can be brought in federal court.

Jurisdictional amount in counterclaims

If the jurisdictional amount is satisfied by the plaintiff's complaint, a compulsory counterclaim not meeting the jurisdictional amount is permitted.

The amount of a counterclaim cannot be aggregated with the plaintiff's claim to satisfy the amount-in-controversy requirement.

Law Essentials: Civil Procedure

Structure of the United States court systems

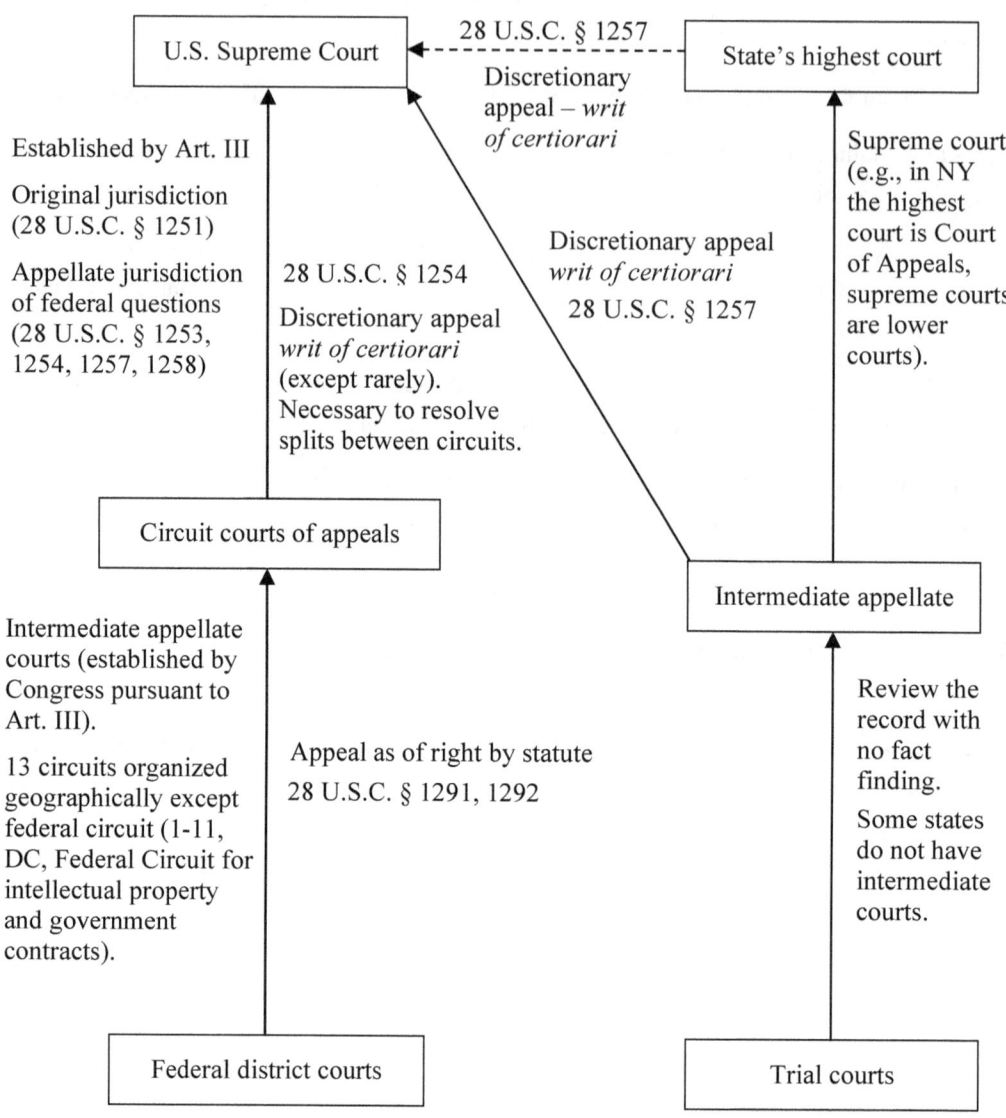

Supplemental Jurisdiction

Supplemental jurisdiction rules

Under 28 U.S.C. § 1367(a), a federal district court generally has supplemental jurisdiction over claims related to the claim upon which federal jurisdiction is founded, which form part of the same *case or controversy*.

Thus, a claim under state antitrust law could be brought in the federal court as a count in the same complaint, which alleges a claim under the federal antitrust law.

The federal court can try a state claim under supplemental jurisdiction even if the count brought under the federal claim is dismissed.

Under *Gibbs*, the federal district court has the discretion to exercise supplemental jurisdiction under 28 U.S.C. § 1367 if:

1) there must be a federal claim (i.e., Constitution, a federal statute, or treaty) and

2) the non-federal claim arises from a "common nucleus of operative fact" such that a plaintiff would ordinarily be expected to try them in one judicial proceeding.

Exceptions to supplemental jurisdiction

1367(b) is an exception to 1367(a): no supplemental jurisdiction if the jurisdiction was a diversity case.

If jurisdiction establishing a claim is a diversity claim, a second claim cannot be brought even if part of the same case or controversy.

The reason for exceptions to supplemental jurisdiction is because 1367(b) should not undermine the complete diversity rule & *Strawbridge*.

1367(c): federal district court can decide not to exercise supplemental jurisdiction if:

1) it raises a complicated question of state law,

2) the claim substantially predominates over the claim or claims over which the district court has original jurisdiction,

3) the district court has dismissed all claims over which it has original jurisdiction, or

4) in exceptional circumstances, there are other compelling reasons for declining jurisdiction.

Notes for active learning

Removal Jurisdiction

Prerequisites to removal – federal subject matter

If the plaintiff could have brought the action in federal court originally, the defendant may remove a civil action brought in a state court to the federal district court.

A federal question raised in defense or counterclaim is not a basis for removal.

The court looks only to the complaint to determine if federal question jurisdiction is present.

The pleadings determine the question of federal jurisdiction, which gives the right to remove as of the time of filing the petition for removal.

If diversity is the basis for federal jurisdiction, the diversity must exist when the original action was filed in state court *and* when the petition for removal was filed.

Only the defendant can remove

Once filing suit in state court, a plaintiff cannot change their mind and remove the case to federal court.

The right to remove is vested only in the defendant.

Diversity cases are not removable if any defendants are citizens of the state in which such action is brought.

For example, if a plaintiff of state A sues a defendant of state B in a state B state court, B may not remove the case to federal court if there is no federal question.

A suit involving a federal question is removable even by a resident defendant.

Separate and independent claim

If an otherwise non-removable state claim is joined with a removable separate and independent federal claim in the state court action, the entire case may be removed to the federal district court.

In its discretion, the federal court may determine all issues or may remand the non-removable claims if state law predominates.

Procedure for removal

Plaintiff may bring suit in the court of their choice if jurisdiction and venue are proper.

Removal is an exception since it provides the defendant with an option to remove a case from state to federal court.

Only the defendant can remove a case.

All defendants must agree to remove the case (i.e., unanimity).

Note, there are strict limitations in the statute and case law regarding which cases may be removed and to which court.

Removal is a one-way street: it only goes from state to federal.

The defendant must file a verified petition for removal in the federal court within 30 days after the case becomes removable and must serve all state court parties with that petition.

The proper venue for a removed action is the district where the state action is pending.

28 U.S.C. § 1447(c): a motion to remand the case from a defect (other than subject matter jurisdiction) must be made within 30 days after the notice of removal has been filed.

A motion to remand may be brought for lack of subject matter jurisdiction at any time during litigation before a final judgment is entered.

Once a case has been removed to federal and remanded back to the state, the motion to remand cannot be appealed.

A plaintiff can file a motion to remand based on the federal court lacking subject matter jurisdiction OR requirements for proper removal were NOT followed.

28 U.S.C. § 1446(b): the notice of removal shall be filed within 30 days from the defendant's receipt of the initial complaint.

If the case stated by the initial pleading is not removable, a defendant may file a notice of removal at any point during the litigation that the case becomes removable.

The defendant shall have 30 days to file a notice of removal from the date the case became removable.

28 U.S.C. § 1446(d): once a case has been removed from state to federal court, the state court shall proceed no further unless and until the case is remanded.

Judgments and orders issued by the state court continue to be in force.

Remand

If the case does not qualify for federal court, the federal court can remand to state court.

The federal court must remand the case to the state court if, before final judgment, it appears that the case was removed improvidently and without jurisdiction.

Jurisdiction Over Persons and Property

Statutory limits of jurisdiction

The issue of *personal jurisdiction* is present in litigation in federal courts.

Generally, such courts have the same personal jurisdiction as the state courts in the state where the federal court is located.

For example, in statutory interpleader actions, jurisdiction extends to the entire United States.

Relationship between defendant and forum state

Personal jurisdiction can be based on the four relationships between the defendant and the forum state:

1) domicile,

2) consent,

3) physical appearance (or service on agent),

4) minimum contacts.

Notes for active learning

Service of Process and Notice

Summons and complaint

Federal Rules of Civil Procedure specify the delivery of the summons and complaint.

Every paper must be served on the opposing party.

Rule 5 governs the delivery of later papers (usually first-class mail).

The *complaint* is the assertion of legal claims.

A *summons* is a court-issued document asserting the court's authority over the defendant.

Adequate notice

Rules for the first delivery are more stringent because the plaintiff must provide the defendant with adequate notice of the pending lawsuit.

Even if service is proper, the court will likely be sympathetic to the defendant and not enforce the *default judgment*.

Mullane (1950) establishes what is necessary for adequate notice for judicial proceedings.

Just because a newspaper advertisement satisfies the statute does not mean it is constitutionally sufficient.

The plaintiff should notify the trustee so they can protect the common interests of beneficiaries.

If it is unreasonable to contact unknown trustees, a paper advertisement is adequate.

Rule 4(c)(2) permits a person over 18 and not a party to the case to deliver the summons.

Rule 4(d) allows the defendant to waive personal service.

Personal and corporate service

Rule 4(e)(2) permits personal service by leaving a copy at the usual place of abode with some person of suitable age who resides therein or delivering it to an agent authorized by appointment or by law to receive service of process.

Service to a corporation can be by personal service to an appointed agent, officer, or managing agent.

Notes for active learning

Venue, *Forum Non Conveniens* and Transfer

Purpose and waiver

Venue rules fix the proper place for the trial of an action over which several courts could exercise jurisdiction.

Venue rules are based on convenience and an effort to distribute cases among trial courts.

Improper venue must be raised affirmatively by the defendant by 1) a motion to dismiss or 2) an answer to the complaint. If not, the right is waived.

Venue rules

In diversity and federal question cases, proper venue in the federal court exists in any district in which either:

1) a defendant resides, if all the defendants reside in the same state, or
2) a "substantial" part of the events or property, which are the basis of the claim or can be found, respectively.

In diversity cases, the venue is proper in any district in which "*the defendants are subject to personal jurisdiction at the time the action commenced.*"

In federal question cases, the venue is proper in any district "in which any defendant may be found," but only "if there is no district in which the action may be otherwise brought."

This situation occurs when the defendants do not reside in the same state, and there is no state in which a "substantial" part of the claim arose.

Residence for venue purposes

For venue, *residence* is the state where the plaintiff is a citizen.

Some courts consider venue proper in a state where a second home is located.

An alien may be sued in any district and cannot use the defense of lack of venue.

The venue for a corporation is in any judicial district that can constitutionally assert personal jurisdiction.

The venue for an unincorporated association (e.g., a partnership) is wherever it is doing business.

Transfer – improper venue

If an action is commenced in the wrong district, the court can dismiss the case according to a motion to dismiss under rule 12(b)(3).

If it is in the interest of justice, the court may transfer the case to any district in which it could have been brought.

The court can transfer an action where it lacks *in personam* jurisdiction over the defendant to a court with such jurisdiction.

Venue is proper for convenience

Even though venue is proper in the district where an action is brought, the court may, in its discretion, transfer the suit to any district "*where it might have been brought...for the convenience of parties and witnesses, in the interest of justice.*" 28 U.S.C. § 1404(a).

The phrase "*where it might have been brought*" limits transfer to a district where the plaintiff could have brought the action when the suit was initiated.

Forum non conveniens

Forum non conveniens allows dismissal by a court if it would be an unfair or inconvenient forum.

An action will be dismissed for *forum non conveniens* if the appropriate forum is a state court or a court in a foreign country.

Law Applied by Federal Courts

Vertical choice of law

In federal court diversity cases, state law applies unless the Constitution or Congressional Statute contradicts this principle.

State law could include statutes, common law, state constitution.

In the absence of a federal statute, state common law applies when a federal court is sitting in diversity jurisdiction.

In the absence of a federal statute or a contrary provision in the Constitution, federal courts must follow state law in diversity cases.

State law was defined to include state common law (*Erie Railroad Co. v. Tompkins*, 1938); *Erie* relies on the 10th Amendment.

Erie established the current foundation of diversity jurisdiction in federal district courts.

If there is a conflict between a federal statute (or US Constitution) and state law, the federal court in a diversity case must use federal law (i.e., Supremacy Clause).

Congress passed the rules enabling act (i.e., Federal Rules of civil procedure), federal courts generally follow the federal rules in diversity cases even if there are contrary state procedures.

Horizontal choice of law

Addresses which law applies to different state laws.

> For torts, the federal district court uses state law where the injury occurred.

> For contracts, the federal district court uses state law where the contract was signed.

A court in another jurisdiction (federal courts or another state court) looks at the lower court decisions and *predicts* how the state's supreme court would rule.

Certification is the process where a federal district court has the state supreme court certify the law by resolving questions from other lower courts in the jurisdiction.

Federal courts and other state courts can request the state supreme court to answer how they would resolve the law.

Some states will only certify requests from Federal Appeals Courts.

Notes for active learning

Pretrial Procedures

Preliminary injunctions and temporary restraining orders

A party may seek a preliminary injunction before a trial on the merits.

Rule 65(a) requires that a preliminary injunction may not be issued without notice to the adverse party.

A temporary restraining order (TRO) is granted by a court when necessary to prevent irreparable harm or injury arising before a preliminary injunction hearing.

Interlocutory injunctions

An injunction is an equitable remedy by which a person is ordered to act (or refrain from acting) in a specified manner.

Interlocutory injunctions are granted to maintain the status quo until a trial on the merits.

Pleadings

Rule 3 pertains to the commencement of a civil action by filing a complaint.

Historically, the rules were strict with pleadings, and if different in court than the pleading, the case was dismissed (variance).

Notice Pleading does not have to allege all facts, but the facts of the cause of action being alleged need to support the cause of action.

The pleading alleges sufficient facts to put the defendant on notice of the claim against them.

Rule 8 requires that the complaint sets out the allegation of facts in numbered paragraphs.

Rule 8(e)(2) allows the plaintiff to plead more than one version of the claim because of the lack of time to discover facts and develop applicable legal theories.

Three Requirements for Federal Complaints (Rule 8):

    1) Jurisdictional allegations—subject matter;

    2) A *"short and plain statement of the claim showing that the pleader is entitled to relief"* (*notice pleading*) – the complaint only needs enough details to put the defendant on notice;

    3) Demand for judgment (e.g., monetary damages).

Special Pleadings (fraud or mistake) are covered by 9(b): the complaint must identify a specific individual who said the fraud or mistake and what they said.

An allegation of fraud needs specificity because it is easy to allege, difficult to defend because the defendant needs to disprove a negative, and it is a damaging accusation,

In response to a complaint, within 21 days of service of process, Rule 8(b) requires the defendant to prepare an answer (also a pleading) by numbering the responses to the allegations and responding to each averment:

1) Affirmative defense: statute of limitations would appear in the answer, and at the end of the answer, the defendant would list affirmative defenses.

   (a) Counterclaim: at the end of the answer, assert counterclaims and list the Answer and Third-party complaints.

   (b) Bring in other parties as defendants.

   (c) A third-party complaint is when a defendant sues another not listed in the complaint

   (d) Cross-complaint is one defendant suing another defendant.

2) Motion to dismiss: filed alleging the lack of grounds for personal, subject matter jurisdiction, or venue.

Rule 12(b) defenses may be raised by motion or answer:

1) lack of subject matter jurisdiction (raised at any time),

2) lack of personal jurisdiction (waivable; must be pleaded in the first response),

3) improper venue (waivable; must be pleaded in the first response),

4) insufficiency of process (waivable; must be pleaded in the first response),

5) insufficiency of service of process (waivable; must be pleaded in the first response),

6) failure to state a claim (may be raised at any time during trial), and

7) failure to join an indispensable party (may be raised at any time during trial).

Counterclaims and crossclaims

Counterclaim is a claim against an opposing party (other side of the *v.*), filed as part of the defendant's answer.

Compulsory counterclaim arises from the same transaction or occurrence as the plaintiff's claim. Must be filed in the pending case or waived.

Permissive counterclaim does not arise from the same transaction or occurrence as the plaintiff's claim.

Crossclaims are claims against a co-party (same side of the *v.*).

A crossclaim filed by one defendant against another will not defeat diversity because the exception to the rule applies only to claims filed by plaintiffs.

Amended and supplemental pleadings

Rule 15(a) entitles a party to amend pleading (complaint or answer) once before the responsive pleading is served.

If the pleading is one to which no responsive pleading is permitted, and the action has not been placed on the trial calendar, the party may amend it within 20 days after it was served.

A party shall plead in response to an amended pleading within the time remaining for a response to the original pleading or within 10 days after service of the amended pleading, whichever period is longer.

The plaintiff may amend a pleading after the defendant filed a motion to dismiss under Rule 12(b)(6) as a motion and not an answer.

The defendant must respond to the amended complaint within 10 days or the time remaining before the pleading was amended

The defendant has a right to amend the answer because it is a pleading to which no responsive pleading is permitted, and the party has 20 days to correct it.

If a party waits too long to amend, the party must file a motion to ask the court's permission to amend the complaint.

Rule 15(c) addresses the statute of limitations and joining a new party or adding a new claim.

Rule 15(c)(2): an amendment to add a claim after the statute of limitations expired relates back only if it illuminates factual details, changes the legal theory, or adds another claim arising out of the same transaction, occurrence, or conduct.

Relation back is denied for those amendments based on entirely different facts, transactions, or occurrences.

Rule 15(c)(3): an amendment to add a new party after the statute of limitations has run.

This amendment is only allowed after the statute of limitations expires if the defendant would not be prejudiced and should have known that, but for a mistake, the party would have been named a defendant.

Rule 15(d): supplemental pleadings set forth events occurring after a pleading is filed for events that occurred after the original pleading was filed.

Supplemental pleadings do not include facts that occurred before the original filing but which were discovered after filing.

Supplemental pleadings update the dispute by bringing such new facts to the court's attention even if they change the relief sought or add additional parties.

Supplemental pleadings are allowed only with the court's permission.

Rule 11 – Ethical Restraints in Pleadings

Veracity of pleadings

Rule 11 (the veracity of pleadings) requires attorneys (or *pro se* litigants) to sign all papers (except discovery documents) certifying:

> the paper is not for an improper purpose (e.g., harass, cause unnecessary delay, needlessly to increase the cost of litigation),

> legal contentions are warranted by law or by a nonfrivolous argument for extending, modifying, reversing existing law, or for establishing new law,

> factual contentions and denials have evidentiary support, and

> the denials of factual contentions are warranted on evidence.

Rule 11 applies to pleadings, motions, and paper representations submitted to the court.

Certification is continuous, so if an attorney argues a point plead, they re-certify the above.

Nonfrivolous claims

A party cannot bring a claim certain they cannot win (challenging a Supreme Court decision).

However, this is not frivolous after a judicial turnover, or the previous bench decision was narrow. Must identify allegations of support likely from discovery *vs.* those already supported.

Sanctions for violations

Sanctions (monetary or non-monetary) may be levied to deter repeated bad conduct.

Safe Harbor Rule: if the other party violates rule 11, a motion can be filed for sanctions on the party and request correction before filing the motion with the court.

There is no safe harbor requirement when the court itself initiates sanctions.

Notes for active learning

Pretrial Motions

Rule 12 pre-answer motions

Rule 12(a)(4): if the pre-answer motion is denied, the respondent has 14 days to file an answer (unless the court sets a different time).

If the pre-answer motion is accepted, an answer may not be required.

After filing the pre-answer motion, there is an ongoing duty to answer until motion is decided.

Rule 12(b) and the special appearance rule require a prompt challenge to personal jurisdiction.

Rule 12(b) allows other defenses to be raised at the same time while a special appearance consents to the jurisdiction of the court.

A defendant can make these motions before filing an answer.

Rule 12(b)(1): dismiss for lack of subject matter jurisdiction – when the court lacks the statutory or constitutional power to adjudicate the case.

Rule 12(b)(4): object to process (e.g., the summons).

Rule 12(b)(5): insufficient service (e.g., manner the summons was served).

Rule 12(b)(6): goes to the merits of the case (i.e., failure to state a claim), and the law does not provide a remedy.

Amending the complaint

Then, the plaintiff can probably amend the complaint.

Rule 12(b)(6): modern version of *demurrer*: even if all facts as pleaded are true, the law supplies no relief.

The court will only look at the complaint and assume facts are true and ask what remedy is available; if none, motion granted

Rule 12(b)(7): failure to join an indispensable party (i.e., cannot adjudicate without violating the rights of a third party).

Many of the above deficiencies are curable (e.g., the court can instruct the plaintiff to serve properly, add the third party).

Motions do not suspend discovery.

However, motion can be made to stay discovery until the motion is decided.

If a motion is made for lack of personal jurisdiction, the litigation proceeds through discovery until the motion is decided.

Most jurisdictions require a brief (i.e., reasons for motion) with the pre-answer motions.

Removal is not a responsive pleading.

After removal, pre-answer motions available are still at the beginning of the suit.

Joinder

Rule 8: joinder of claims for parties

Rule 8 governs counterclaims: pleadings for claims for relief with counterclaims and crossclaims.

Joinder of claims for parties:

1) Some common questions of law or fact.

2) Arising from the same transaction or occurrence.

Counterclaims

Rule 13(a) compulsory counterclaim: from the same set of events.

Rule 13(b) permissive counterclaim: if arising from different events.

Rule 13(b): once a defendant has been sued with a crossclaim, the defendant can invoke compulsory and permissive counterclaims.

Crossclaims

Rule 13(h): additional parties to a crossclaim for related claims.

Rule 18(a): plaintiff or defendant asserting a claim may join claims, even if unrelated to underlying facts, against an opposing party.

Once a proper crossclaim is done, additional unrelated crossclaims can be added without violating subject matter jurisdiction.

Rule 18(b): joinder of contingent claims.

A party may join two claims even though one is dependent on the disposition of the other.

Joinder of parties

Rule 19: pertains to the joinder of parties. Requires individual defendants must be ordered by the court to be added into a suit.

This motion for joinder may be raised in a pre-answer motion.

Rule 20(a): joinder of parties from common questions or facts in the occurrence of the action, the defendant and plaintiff can be joined.

Proper joinder under Rule 20(a), Rule 18 permits adding unrelated claims.

Rule 42(b) authorizes a judge to do separate trials for unrelated claims. If the claim is a diversity claim, and a non-diverse party's joinder destroys diversity, the court decides if the party is necessary and, if so, if a party is indispensable and still a remedy exists for the plaintiff (in state court).

Discovery

Automatic disclosure

Discovery is a lawyer-driven process to investigate a claim and compel documents.

Rule 26(a)(1) pertains to initial disclosures.

Rule 26 requires disclosure without waiting for a discovery request.

Opposing counsel must turn over at the beginning of litigation.

1) witnesses that support a position in the case
2) any document that will be used to support the case
3) describe the adversary nature of damages
4) insurance agreements to determine the policy limits

Rule 26 requires parties to disclose all information "*then reasonably available*" that is not privileged or protected as work product.

Rule 26 has provisions allowing stipulation of the parties (or court order) to modify some disclosure requirements.

Before making disclosures, a party must make a reasonable inquiry into the facts.

Privileges exist as recognition that it is more important to protect this communication than reveal this information.

Courts have discretion, so the Appellate level standard for review is an *abuse of discretion*.

For a good cause shown, a court can allow the discovery of any matter "*relevant to the subject matter*" involved.

Information need not be admissible to be discoverable if it is "reasonably calculated *to lead to* the discovery of admissible evidence"—evidence might lead you to admissible evidence.

Rule 33 allows a party to provide access to files, but there could be privileged information in these files.

Common objections of discovery

Rule 26(b)(1): discovery regarding any matter not privileged is relevant to any party's claim or defense.

Not all relevant information is admissible but may lead to admissible evidence.

The broader the pleadings in the complaint, the broader is discovery.

If it is allowed for the opposing side to inspect all documents, privileged and work product are waived.

Rule 26(b)(2): the court can limit discovery.

Parties can object and receive protective orders.

Limitations on discovery include:

    1) unduly burdensome

    2) cumulative

    3) available elsewhere

Rule 26(b)(3): pertains to documents and tangible things.

For example, work product (e.g., notes on preparing for litigation, legal judgments, strategies) is protected.

Rule 26(b)(5): must articulate why using privilege as much as possible (i.e., not disclosing).

Discovery sanctions

Rule 26(g): discovery (including discovery responses) must be:

> Consistent with the rules and warranted by existing law or good faith extension, modification, or reversal of existing law.

> Not interposed for any improper purpose (e.g., to harass, cause unnecessary delay, increase litigation costs).

> Not unreasonable or unduly burdensome or expensive given the needs of the case.

Rule 26(g)(3): failure to comply with discovery requests can result in sanctions against the attorney or party, including payment of the opponent's expenses (i.e., attorneys' fees) due to violations.

Depositions

Rule 30 covers depositions: witness testimony under oath.

Depositions can be taken from anyone.

Advantages of depositions: uncoached testimony, can ask follow-up questions, and observe a person's reaction to the questions.

Disadvantages of depositions: expensive, difficult to plan, have to study the case to do effectively (a reason why depositions are usually taken late in the case).

Sometimes depositions are taken early in the case before the witness knows enough about the case to be aware of what information to hide.

Usually, a witness comes to trial, but when this is not possible, a videotape of the deposition may be used after being screened for objections.

At deposition, objections are noted, but answers must be given.

The deponent can refuse to answer privileged questions.

Rule 30(d)(4): prohibits harassing or embarrassing questions.

Interrogatories

Rule 33: interrogatories are written questions (limited to 25 interrogatories unless the court approves more).

Interrogatories must be answered from memory or records (e.g., files).

Interrogatories are valuable to determine whom to depose (e.g., determine the identity of people that may have information).

Interrogatories are often written by lawyers and answered by lawyers under oath.

Interrogatories elicit facts (e.g., names and addresses of witnesses, doctors' bills).

Interrogatories are limited in number, so multi-part questions are problematic.

No follow-up questions are permitted.

Interrogatories are for parties of the suit and not for witnesses.

Often, the sequence is interrogatories first, document requests, and depositions after evaluating earlier information.

Production of documents

Rule 34 covers requests for the production of documents sent to parties in the case.

Requests for the production of documents require a subpoena for non-parties.

Witnesses and documents can be obtained by subpoena.

If in a foreign language, the producing party must translate.

Physical and mental exams

Rule 36: covers physical and mental exams.

A court order is needed for the physical or mental exams of a party.

Personal injury cases permit the physical exam but may be limited in scope.

Physical exams for witnesses are excluded, but records may be subpoenaed.

Request for admissions

Rule 36: requests for admissions: to avoid litigating specific points.

Rule 37(a): when someone fails to comply with a motion to compel.

37(a)(2)(b): applies in the context of a motion to compel.

A motion to compel is filed after an opponent has failed to comply with discovery.

Must confer with an opponent before filing the motion to compel.

The court may award fees to the party who successfully pursues or defends against such an action.

Rule 37(b)(2): does not allow sanctions for interfering with discovery until there is an effort to work it out since the defendant may resist if the item requested is too burdensome.

Adjudication Without a Trial

Voluntary dismissal

Rule 41 covers dismissals.

Plaintiff may dismiss an action without a court order by filing:

> i) a notice of dismissal before the opposing party serves an answer or a motion for summary judgment; or
>
> ii) a stipulation of dismissal signed by parties who appeared.

Unless specified otherwise, the dismissal is without prejudice.

If the plaintiff previously dismissed a federal- or state-court action based on or including the same claim, a notice of dismissal operates as an adjudication on the merits.

Except as provided in Rule 41(a)(1), a plaintiff's action for dismissal is only by court order, on terms the court considers proper.

If a defendant has pleaded a counterclaim before being served with the plaintiff's motion to dismiss, the action may be dismissed over the defendant's objection only if the counterclaim can remain pending for independent adjudication.

Involuntary dismissal

If the plaintiff fails to prosecute or to comply with these rules or court order, a defendant may move to dismiss the action.

Unless the dismissal order states otherwise, a dismissal operates as an adjudication on the merits, except:

> lack of jurisdiction,
>
> improper venue, or
>
> failure to join a party under Rule 19.

Dismissing counterclaims, crossclaim or third-party claims

A claimant's voluntary dismissal under Rule 41(a)(1)(A)(i) must be made:

    1) before a responsive pleading is served, or

    2) if there is no responsive pleading before evidence is introduced at a hearing or trial.

If a plaintiff who previously dismissed an action in any court files an action based on or including the same claim against the same defendant, the court:

    1) may order the plaintiff to pay some costs of the previous action; and

    2) may stay the proceedings until the plaintiff has complied.

Pretrial Conference and Order

Pretrial conferences

The court may hold pretrial conferences to expedite the trial and encourage settlement.

Pretrial Disclosures: at least 30 days before trial, a party must disclose to the other parties and file with the court a list of:

- witnesses to be called at trial,
- witnesses that may be called if the need arises,
- witnesses whose testimony will be presented by deposition
- transcript of pertinent portions of the deposition, and
- documents or exhibits they expect to offer if needed.

Evidence or witnesses that would be used solely for impeachment need not be disclosed.

Within 14 days after this disclosure, a party may serve objections to the use of the depositions at trial and the admissibility of disclosed documents and exhibits.

Such objections are waived if not made at this point, except for objections that the evidence is irrelevant, prejudicial, or confusing under Federal Rules of Evidence 402 and 403.

Rule 16(b): scheduling conference: the court must (except in classes of cases exempted by local rule) hold a scheduling conference among the parties or counsel.

The conference may be held by telephone, mail, or suitable means.

Within 90 days after the appearance of a defendant and within 120 days after the complaint has been served on a defendant, the court must enter a scheduling order limiting the time for joinder, motions, and discovery.

Rule 26(f) Conference of Parties when planning for discovery: as soon as practicable, and at least 21 days before a scheduling conference is held or the scheduling order required by Rule 16(b) is due, the parties must confer to consider:

- their claims and defenses,
- the possibility of settlement,
- initial disclosures, and
- a discovery plan.

The parties must submit to the court a proposed discovery plan within 14 days after the conference addressing:

> the timing and form of required disclosures,
>
> the subjects on which discovery may be needed,
>
> the timing of and limitations on discovery, and
>
> relevant orders that may be required of the court.

The order may include dates for pretrial conferences, a trial date, and appropriate matters.

A final pretrial conference is held as close to the trial as reasonable.

A final pretrial conference formulates a trial plan, including the admission of evidence.

At least one of the lawyers for each side conducting the trial and unrepresented parties should attend the final pretrial conference.

After a pretrial conference, an order must be entered that controls the subsequent course of events in the case.

Thus, the final pretrial conference order is a blueprint for the trial:

> listing witnesses to be called,
>
> evidence to be presented,
>
> factual and legal issues needing resolution.

The final pretrial conference supersedes the pleadings and may be modified only *for good cause*.

Jury Trials

Right to a jury trial – demand

The right of trial by jury as declared by the Seventh Amendment—or as provided by federal statute—is preserved to the parties inviolate.

On issue triable of right by a jury, a party may demand a jury trial by:

> 1) serving the other parties with a written demand—which may be included in a pleading—no later than 14 days after serving the last pleading; and
>
> 2) filing the demand per Rule 5(d).

Rules 38 and 39 govern the demand for a jury trial.

In its demand, a party may specify the issues tried by a jury; otherwise, it is considered to have demanded a jury trial on all issues triable.

If the party has demanded a jury trial on only some issues, within 14 days after being served with the demand or within a shorter time ordered by the court, any other party may serve a demand for a jury trial on issues triable by jury.

A party waives the right to a jury trial unless its demand is properly served and filed.

A proper demand may be withdrawn only if the parties consent.

These rules do not create a right to a jury trial on issues in a claim that is an admiralty or maritime claim under Rule 9(h).

Selection and composition of juries

Rule 47 addresses selecting jurors.

The court may permit the parties to examine prospective jurors or may itself do so.

If the court examines the jurors, it must permit the parties or their attorneys to make further inquiry it considers proper or must ask additional questions it considers proper.

28 U.S.C. § 1870 requires the court to allow some peremptory challenges (e.g., three for civil trials).

During trial or deliberation, the court may excuse a juror *for good cause*.

Number of jurors, verdict and polling

Rule 48 pertains to the number of jurors, verdict, and polling

A jury must begin with at least 6 and no more than 12 members, and each juror must participate in the verdict unless excused.

Unless the parties stipulate otherwise, the verdict must be unanimous and must be returned by a jury of at least 6 members.

After a verdict is returned but before the jury is discharged, the court must, on a party's request (or may on its own), poll the jurors individually.

If the poll reveals a lack of unanimity or lack of assent by the number of jurors that the parties stipulated to, the court may direct the jury to continue deliberating or order a new trial.

Jury instructions

At the close of the evidence or at an earlier reasonable time that the court orders, a party may file and furnish to every other party written requests for the jury instructions it wants the court to give.

After the close of the evidence, a party may:

> 1) file requests for instructions on issues that could not reasonably have been anticipated by an earlier time that the court set for requests; and

> 2) with the court's permission, file untimely requests for instructions on an issue.

After the close of the evidence, the court:

> 1) must inform the parties of its proposed instructions and proposed action on the requests before instructing the jury and before final jury arguments,

> 2) must allow the parties to object on the record and out of the jury's hearing before instructions or arguments are delivered, and

> 3) may instruct the jury at any time before the jury is discharged.

Instructions to the jury for objections

A party who objects to an instruction (or failure of instruction) must do so on the record.

The record must include the matter precisely objected to and the grounds for the objection.

An objection is timely if:

> 1) a party objects at the opportunity provided under Rule 51(b)(2), or

> 2) a party was not informed of instruction or action on a request before that opportunity to object, and the party objects promptly after learning that the instruction or request will be, or has been, given or refused.

Instructions to the jury preserving a claim of error

A party may assign as error:

> 1) an error in an instruction given if that party properly objected; or

> 2) a failure to give an instruction if that party properly requested it and—unless the court rejected the request in a definitive ruling on the record—also properly objected.

A court may consider a plain error in the instructions that have not been preserved as required by Rule 51(d)(1) if the error affects substantial rights.

Notes for active learning

Motions

Pretrial motions

The sequence of events at trial:

> Opening Statements
>
> Plaintiff's case in chief: the plaintiff has the burden of proof.
>
> Defendant's case: support position of no liability.
>
> Closing Argument
>
> Deliberation

Summary judgment

Rule 56 pertains to Summary Judgment.

Motions for Summary Judgment takes place after discovery, uses evidence from discovery, and tries to get the case disposed of.

Motion granted if evidence does not show plausibility for a jury to find for one party.

The question for summary judgment: is there a genuine issue of material fact?

Convincing Clarity Standard—the more difficult the case is to prove at trial, the more challenging it to survive a summary judgment motion.

The moving party for summary judgment must demonstrate an absence of evidence to support the nonmoving party's case.

If the moving party establishes a lack of evidence, a non-moving party must present specific facts showing a genuine trial issue.

Summary judgment may be granted on parts of the case.

If the defendant prevails on one element of the case, the plaintiff prevails because the plaintiff has the burden of proof on all elements.

If the plaintiff prevails on one element, that element is not at issue during trial.

The plaintiff may plead a legally sufficient case (i.e., survives a Rule 12(b)(6) Motion), but the defendant may have facts that eliminate an essential element.

In such a case, the defendant can file a motion for summary judgment, attach admissible evidence, and a brief explaining the legal meaning.

The plaintiff has a chance to respond to the motion that shows contradicting evidence to establish a factual dispute requiring a jury.

In some cases, sides agree on the facts, and each submits a motion for summary judgment to get a ruling on the legal implication of those facts.

Rule 56(e): when a motion is made, an adverse party cannot just rely on allegations in the complaint.

If an adverse party does not respond, summary judgment will be granted, if appropriate.

If the evidence presented by an opposing party still makes a conclusion doubtful, summary judgment is not appropriate.

Summary Judgment is based on the papers before trial (e.g., motions, briefs, affidavits).

Declaratory judgment

Rule 57 addresses declaratory judgment (i.e., a binding judgment from a court defining the legal relationship between parties and their rights in a matter before the court).

The existence of another adequate remedy does not preclude a declaratory judgment that is otherwise appropriate.

A court may order a speedy hearing of a declaratory judgment action. Declaratory Judgment is a mechanism for a party to bring suit to itself to determine its liabilities and rights.

If the party expects to be sued, they can bring the matter to the court to hear its opinion on how it would rule if they were sued if they performed in a particular manner.

Courts only grant declaratory judgments when there is an immediately focused controversy between the parties.

Directed verdict – judgment as a matter of law (JMOL)

Rule 50: *Motions of Judgment as Matter of Law* (JMOL): a motion made by a party during the trial, claiming the opposing party has insufficient evidence to reasonably support its case.

Rule 50(a): *Directed Verdict*: verdict rendered by a jury upon instruction by the judge that they must bring in that verdict because one of the parties has not proved their case as a matter of law.

The JMOL has replaced directed verdicts in federal courts.

Direct Verdict motion is raised after a party has had an opportunity to present their case. The non-moving party has presented all evidence:

    must be made before the case presented to the jury, and

    must specify the basis for the motion.

A motion for judgment as a matter of law (JMOL) may be made at any time before the case is submitted to the jury.

Summary judgment versus directed verdict

Summary judgment is a pretrial procedure. Summary judgment motions assert that there are no issues of fact for a jury (or court) to decide. The essential facts are uncontested, and therefore one side is entitled to prevail as a matter of law (i.e., the application of law to facts). Either the plaintiff or the defense may make a summary judgment motion.

Directed verdict is a trial procedure. It is typically a defense motion brought at the close of the plaintiff's case and asserts that upon the facts presented (whether contested or not), the plaintiff is not entitled to judgment because:

1) the plaintiff has not put forth sufficient proof to establish the elements of their claim or

2) the plaintiff's claim fails as a matter of law (same as summary judgment) because either the cause of action is not recognized at law or the correct legal interpretation of facts defeats the plaintiff's claim.

For example, a real estate contract dispute is not in writing and therefore fails because of the statute of the frauds.

There are similarities between summary judgment and directed verdict as both can be used to determine the case as a matter of law. Often, issues before the court on directed verdict were presented (or could have been) as summary judgment motions.

The main difference is that a directed verdict motion asserts the failure to establish *facts supporting the elements of a claim*, which is an evidentiary problem at trial.

There are practical or tactical reasons why a litigant may (or may not) make a summary judgment motion before trial instead of a directed verdict at trial. However, these reasons have more to do with trial strategy.

Seventh Amendment considerations

How can this be balanced with the Seventh Amendment?

1) Right to a jury trial shall be preserved as existed in 1791,

2) Juries determine the facts, and if there are no facts to decide, then not taking anything away from the jury.

The plaintiff cannot make the motion immediately after presenting their case because the defendant has no chance to present the case yet, but the defendant could since the plaintiff had their chance to plead their case.

A plaintiff suing several different defendants because not sure which one is liable; the plaintiff puts on evidence that 2 of 3 defendants are liable.

However, the third defendant may move for a directed verdict because the plaintiff has not proved anything for that defendant to be liable. No reasonable jury could find for the plaintiff.

The court grants a motion for a directed verdict (i.e., JMOL) if no reasonable jury could find in favor of the nonmoving party (federal approach).

If the court does not grant a motion for judgment as a matter of law made under Rule 50(a), the court is considered to have submitted the action to the jury subject to the court's later deciding the legal questions raised by the motion.

Why would a judge grant a motion before going to the jury?

> 1) Preserve the Seventh Amendment by not reexamining the jury's findings; just renew the decision on the motion as a matter of law.
>
> 2) Allows a party to fix the problem with the case.

The plaintiff can reopen the case to present new evidence.

Standards of review

Standards of review are the same under Rule 50(a) and Rule 50(b).

Scintilla test: even if only little (*scintilla*) evidence in support, it goes to the jury.

Plaintiff's evidence standard: assessing whether a jury can hear the case, only look at the plaintiff's evidence.

Federal Standards: viewing the plaintiff's case in a most favorable light *and* considering all uncontradicted evidence of the defendant (inferences to favor the plaintiff).

A judgment as a matter of law is reviewed *de novo* on appeal.

More deference is given to the lower court, which conducted the entire trial.

In a bench trial, a motion is made under Rule 52.

Under Rule 52, a fundamentally different argument that evidence has not met the burden of proof (judge is fact finder).

JMOL motion is before the jury so that the other side can address issues.

JMOL is a judgment because the court heard the merits of the case.

Judgment notwithstanding verdict (JNOV)

Rule 50(a) requires the JMOL to be filed *first*.

After the verdict, the JMOL can be renewed.

Rule 50(b): *Judgment notwithstanding the verdict* (JNOV).

The *difference* between a judgment as a matter of law (JMOL) / directed verdict is that the motion for the judgment notwithstanding the verdict (JNOV) is made *after* the jury renders a verdict.

For example, the case goes to the jury, and the jury finds for the other party.

The moving party asks the judge to overrule what the jury concluded.

The standard to issue a JMOL is whether a reasonable jury decided this way. If a reasonable jury could not have decided like this, the judge might enter a JNOV.

Rule: only where there is a complete absence of probative facts to support the conclusion reached does a reversible error appear.

If there is an evidentiary basis for the jury's verdict, the jury is free to disregard whatever facts are inconsistent with its conclusion.

Plaintiff appeals and review is *de novo*; if reversed, the matter goes to a new jury.

If the plaintiff wins, the judge orders a new trial.

If the appeals court agrees, the case is remanded to reinstate the judgment on the original verdict.

If the jury gives excessive damages, the judge can ask the plaintiff to reduce (i.e., remittitur) some of the damages.

If not, the court orders a new trial on damages.

If damages too low, the court asks the defendant to pay more (i.e., additur); a new trial might award more.

The reason for the JNOV is to avoid a new trial.

Scenario 1: Judge grants motion before a jury hears the case (JMOL or directed verdict); if reversed on appeal, the case must be tried again.

Scenario 2: Motion for JMOL/directed verdict; judge denies or defers. The case goes to jury; the defendant renews the motion (JNOV) after the jury presents findings; the judge grants the defendant's motion.

If appealed and reversed, judgment entered on the jury's verdict.

Motions for a new trial

If procedural problems (e.g., jury hearing inadmissible evidence) or clear error, a motion for a new trial will be sustained. For example,

> 1) Procedural Issues: if a judge makes a prejudicial mistake like inadmissible evidence, improper jury instructions, improper contacts with the jury, an improper argument to the jury.

> 2) Verdict is clearly wrong; the judge deems seriously erroneous result.

Not deprivation of the Seventh Amendment because it just goes to another jury

Piesco (1990) granted summary judgment and reversed it.

A judge granted Rule 59 motion for a new trial, so no final judgment allowed and no interlocutory appeal.

Must wait for the second trial. If a disfavorable outcome, the plaintiff can appeal the Ruling on the Rule 59 motion, and if reversed, the first trial judgment will be entered or denied, and judgment entered on the second trial

A new trial may be ordered for one defendant (e.g., issue of damages).

The judge could award *remittitur* in which the plaintiff has the option to take less money than the jury granted or go to a new trial.

Instead of saying that no reasonable jury could have rendered this way, the judge decides that it is against the manifest of evidence.

Juries can draw inferences from the evidence, but they must be drawn according to the law.

If inferences are not correctly drawn, despite the manifest of evidence, a new trial can be granted.

Can do partial mistrial – new trial on specific issues.

No later than 28 days after the entry of judgment—or if the motion addresses a jury issue not decided by a verdict, no later than 28 days after the jury was discharged.

The movant may file a renewed motion for judgment as a matter of law and may include an alternative or joint request for a new trial under Rule 59.

In ruling on the renewed motion, the court may:

> 1) allow judgment on the verdict if the jury returned a verdict;

> 2) order a new trial; or

> 3) direct the entry of judgment as a matter of law.

Granting the renewed motion

If the court grants a renewed motion for judgment as a matter of law, the court must conditionally rule on any motion for a new trial by determining whether a new trial should be granted if the judgment is later vacated or reversed.

The court must state the grounds for conditionally granting or denying the motion for a new trial.

Conditional ruling on a motion for a new trial

Conditionally granting the motion for a new trial does not affect the judgment's finality; if the judgment is reversed, the new trial must proceed unless the appellate court orders otherwise.

If the motion for a new trial is conditionally denied, the appellee may assert an error in that denial.

If the judgment is reversed, the case must proceed as the appellate court orders.

Notes for active learning

Verdicts and Judgments

Findings and conclusions by the court

Rule 52 pertains to Findings and Conclusions by the Court.

In an action tried on the facts without a jury or with an advisory jury, the court must find the facts specially and state its conclusions of law separately.

The findings and conclusions may be stated on the record after the close of the evidence or may appear in an opinion or a memorandum of the court's decision.

Judgment must be entered under Rule 58.

In granting or refusing an interlocutory injunction, the court must similarly state the findings and conclusions that support its action.

The court is not required to state findings or conclusions when ruling on a motion under Rule 12 or 56 or, unless these rules provide otherwise, on any other motion.

A master's findings, to the extent adopted by the court, must be considered the court's findings.

A party may question the sufficiency of the evidence supporting the findings, whether or not the party requested findings, objected, moved to amend them, or moved for partial findings.

Whether based on oral or other evidence, findings of fact must not be set aside unless *clearly erroneous*.

The reviewing court must give due regard to the trial court's opportunity to judge the witnesses' credibility.

Amended or additional findings

On a party's motion filed no later than 28 days after the entry of judgment, the court may amend its findings (or make additional findings) and amend the judgment accordingly.

The motion may accompany a motion for a new trial under Rule 59.

Judgment on partial findings

If a party has been fully heard on an issue during a nonjury trial, and the court finds against the party on that issue, the court may enter judgment against the party on a claim or defense that, under controlling law, can be maintained or defeated only with a favorable finding on that issue.

A court may decline to render a judgment until the close of the evidence.

A judgment on partial findings must be supported by findings of fact and conclusions of law as required by Rule 52(a).

Entering judgment

Judgments NOT on merits: subject matter, jurisdiction, personal jurisdiction, venue, improper service of process, failure to join a party.

Judgments on merits:

>summary judgment,
>
>directed verdict,
>
>Rule 12(b)(6) (get chance to amend complaint), or
>
>dismissal for failure to prosecute.

In a state with 12(b)(6) motions not barring the second suit, the suit brought in federal district court will apply the same principles.

The court will probably not grant Rule 60(b) relief as an attempt to avoid *res judicata*.

Rule 58 pertains to entering judgment.

Every judgment and amended judgment must be set out in a separate document, but a separate document is not required for an order disposing of a motion:

>1) for judgment under Rule 50(b),
>
>2) to amend or make additional findings under Rule 52(b),
>
>3) for attorney's fees under Rule 54,
>
>4) for a new trial under Rule 59,
>
>5) to alter or amend the judgment under Rule 59, or
>
>6) for relief under Rule 60.

Subject to Rule 54(b) and unless the court orders otherwise, the clerk must, without awaiting the court's direction, promptly prepare, sign, and enter the judgment when:

>1) the jury returns a general verdict,
>
>2) the court awards only costs or a sum certain, or
>
>3) the court denies relief.

Subject to Rule 54(b), the court must promptly approve the form of the judgment, which the clerk must promptly enter, when:

> 1) the jury returns a special verdict or a general verdict with answers to written questions; or
>
> 2) court grants other relief not described in this subdivision.

For purposes of these rules, judgment is entered at the following times:

> 1) if a separate document is not required, when the judgment is entered in the civil docket under Rule 79(a), or
>
> 2) if a separate document is required, when the judgment is entered in the civil docket under Rule 79(a), and the earlier occurs:
>
>> (a) it is set out in a separate document, or
>>
>> (b) 150 days have run from the entry in the civil docket.

A party may request that judgment be set out in a separate document per Rule 58(a).

Ordinarily, the entry of judgment may not be delayed, nor the time for appeal extended to tax costs or award fees.

If a timely motion for attorney's fees is made under Rule 54(d)(2, the court may act before a notice of appeal has been filed and become effective to order that the motion has the same effect under Federal Rule of Appellate Procedure 4(a)(4) as a timely motion under Rule 59.

Relief from a judgment or order

Rule 60 pertains to Relief from a Judgment or Order.

The court may correct a clerical mistake or a mistake arising from oversight or omission whenever a mistake is found in a judgment, order, or another part of the record.

The court may do so on motion or its own, with or without notice.

After an appeal has been docketed and pending, a mistake may be corrected only with the appellate court's leave.

On motion and just terms, the court may relieve a party or its legal representative from a final judgment, order, or proceeding for the following reasons:

1) mistake, inadvertence, surprise, or excusable neglect,

2) newly discovered evidence that, with reasonable diligence, could not have been discovered in time to move for a new trial under Rule 59(b),

3) fraud (whether intrinsic or extrinsic), misrepresentation, or misconduct by an opposing party,

4) the judgment is void,

5) the judgment has been satisfied, released, or discharged; it is based on an earlier judgment that has been reversed or vacated, or applying it prospectively is no longer equitable, or

6) any other reason that justifies relief.

Claim preclusion – *res judicata*

A plaintiff cannot bring the second cause of action based on the same facts and evidence after an original cause of action has been litigated.

Federal Rules of Civil Procedure are flexible to get the whole case heard *but* very strict about providing a second chance to try the case.

Four requirements for *res judicata*:

1) final judgment,

2) on the merits,

3) claims must be the same,

4) parties must be the same.

Federal district court uses claims about the same transaction or series of transactions like joinder (same set of historical facts).

Therefore, a plaintiff must present all claims in one lawsuit.

An exception applies to cases that statutes direct the subject to federal court (e.g., patents).

For example, if the defendant pleads *res judicata*, it will not prevail because the patent claim could not have brought in state court.

If the plaintiff may sue on the claim in the first suit – *res judicata* applies.

If the court in the first suit never reached merits (no judgment), *res judicata* does not apply.

If suit 1 is in federal court and suit 2 is in state court, suit 2 will be barred if it could have been added to the federal docket under supplemental jurisdiction.

However, if it did offer the suit and it was denied, it will not be barred.

Win or lose, the plaintiff is barred from a second lawsuit on the claim.

If the plaintiff wins, the claim is merged with the judgment.

If the plaintiff lost, the claim becomes barred.

For analysis, consider the same parties as before and claims from the same underlying transaction – focus on the underlying events/facts.

For an error in the first case, appealing the first judgment is the remedy.

If the defendant sues the plaintiff after the plaintiff sued the defendant, it is barred based on the same underlying facts.

Compulsory counterclaim rules are based on *res judicata*.

If a counterclaim is permissive, then not barred.

If crossclaim is permissive, then not barred.

If the defendant impleads a third party, then the defendant sues the third party on the same underlying facts; it is barred because the defendant should have asserted all claims when impleading the third party.

If the plaintiff did not pursue a lawsuit, then barred by failure to prosecute barred by that judgment or dismissal; had a chance to litigate merits and did not pursue – no second chances.

If the defendant defaults, barred because they ignored the merits.

If the law changes, they still cannot litigate because they would still be suing on the same underlying facts.

Federal courts: (majority rule for state courts): when it arises from the same cause of action—transaction, occurrence, or event—it is part of the same claim and cannot litigate it again.

Minority rule (for state courts): if one cause of action gives rise to two different claims, the second claim is not precluded. Claims are different if the nature of the harm done is different (e.g., property damage *vs*. personal injury).

Determine whether subsequent cases involve the same claim.

1) Type of damages: used in a minority of states.

2) Single occurrence (federal courts).

3) Sameness of evidence: to establish liability.

4) Common nucleus of operative facts: restatement definition.

Parties are identical or in privity with the same configuration (parties bound in the dispute).

Privity: whatever benefits the first plaintiff would get from the first lawsuit would benefit the second plaintiff, so the claim precluded. For example, a trustee brings a claim for the beneficiary's benefit; the beneficiary cannot bring the same claim against the same defendant.

Privity: rights were already exhausted because the previous plaintiff already exhausted them; For example, trying the same case again with a different person standing in.

Class action: person part of a class action, even though not named, cannot bring a claim independently; the legal relationship between litigant and party, not a litigant.

The same configuration of parties: the plaintiff must be the same in the second case.

The plaintiff must be the one to sue the defendant in both cases; it is not the same configuration if the defendant initiates a suit.

Valid final judgment: valid unless no jurisdiction or venue issues; it becomes a final judgment after the trial court is done with the matter.

On the merits – had the opportunity to have the substance heard:

1) summary judgment (SJ),

2) judgment as a matter of law (JMOL),

3) judgment notwithstanding the verdict (JNOV).

If dismissed for lack of jurisdiction, cannot impose claim preclusion because the issue was not tried on the merits.

Dismissed because of other elements not due to merits, have not had a day in court.

Rule 12(6) motion to dismiss for *failure to state a claim*: court dismisses the claim with prejudice (after the amended complaint).

Some states hold that dismissal for failure to state a claim is on the merits because no claim was stated.

Issue preclusion – collateral estoppel

Prevents litigation of particular issues that were litigated and determined in the first case.

If the first case argues A, B, C, and D, and the second case argues A, X, Y, and Z, defendant A cannot be sued again since they were included in the prior suit.

Elements of analysis:

    Was the same issue litigated and determined in the first case?

    Was the issue essential to the judgment in the first case?

    Was the holding on that issue embodied in a valid, final judgment on the merits?

    Is the preclusion being exercised against an appropriate party?

    Is the preclusion being asserted by an appropriate party (mutuality issue)?

Notes for active learning

Appeals and Review with Government as a Party

Appeal as of right

Rule 4 applies to Appeal as of Right.

In a civil case, except as provided in Rules 4(a)(1)(B), 4(a)(4), and 4(c), the notice of appeal required by Rule 3 must be filed with the district clerk within 30 days after entry of the judgment or order appealed from.

Any party may file the notice of appeal within 60 days after entry of the judgment or order appealed from if one of the parties is:

1) the United States;

2) a United States agency;

3) a United States officer or employee sued in an official capacity; or

4) a current or former United States officer or employee sued in an individual capacity for an act or omission occurring in connection with official duties (including instances in which the United States represents that person when the judgment or order is entered or files the appeal for that person).

An appeal from an order granting or denying an application for a writ of error *coram nobis* (i.e., *a fundamental error of manifest injustice*) is an appeal in a civil case for purposes of Rule 4(a).

A notice of appeal is filed after the court announces a decision or order but before the entry of judgment or order is treated as filed on the date of and after the entry.

If one party timely files a notice of appeal, any other party may file a notice of appeal within 14 days after the date when the first notice was filed or within the time prescribed by Rule 4(a), whichever period ends later.

Notes for active learning

Appeals and Review for Civil Cases

Effect of a motion on a notice of appeal

If a party files in the district court any of the following motions under the Federal Rules of Civil Procedure – and does within the time allowed – the time to file an appeal runs for all parties from the entry of the order disposing of the last remaining motion:

1) for judgment under Rule 50(b);

2) to amend or make additional factual findings under Rule 52(b), whether or not granting the motion would alter the judgment;

3) for attorney's fees under Rule 54 if the district court extends the time to appeal under Rule 58;

4) to alter or amend the judgment under Rule 59;

5) for a new trial under Rule 59; or

6) for relief under Rule 60 if the motion is filed no later than 28 days after the judgment is entered.

If a party files a notice of appeal after the judgment – but before the court disposes of motions listed in Rule 4(a)(4)(A) – the notice becomes effective to appeal a judgment or order, in whole or part, when the order disposing of the last remaining motion is entered.

A party intending to challenge an order disposing of any motion listed in Rule 4(a)(4)(A), or a judgment's alteration or amendment upon such a motion, must file a notice of appeal or an amended notice of appeal – in compliance with Rule 3(c) – within the time prescribed by this Rule measured from the entry of the order disposing of the last such remaining motion.

No additional fee is required to file an amended notice.

Motion for extension of time

The district court may extend the time to file a notice of appeal if:

1) a party so moves no later than 30 days after the time prescribed by this Rule 4(a) expires; and

2) regardless of whether its motion is filed within the 30 days after the time prescribed by Rule 4(a), that party shows excusable neglect or good cause.

A motion filed before the expiration of the time prescribed in Rule 4(a)(1) or (3) may be *ex parte* unless the court requires otherwise.

If the motion is filed after the prescribed time expiration, notice must be given to the other parties per local rules.

No extension under Rule 4(a)(5) may exceed 30 days after the prescribed time or 14 days after the date when the order granting the motion is entered, whichever is later.

Reopening the time to file an appeal

The district court may reopen the time to file an appeal for 14 days after the date when its order to reopen is entered, but only if the following conditions are satisfied:

1) the court finds that the moving party did not receive notice under Federal Rule of Civil Procedure 77(d) of the entry of the judgment or order sought to be appealed within 21 days after entry;

2) the motion is filed within 180 days after the judgment or order is entered or within 14 days after the moving party receives notice under Federal Rule of Civil Procedure 77(d) of the entry, whichever is earlier; and

3) the court finds that no party would be prejudiced.

Entry defined

A judgment or order is entered for purposes of this Rule 4(a):

1) if Federal Rule of Civil Procedure 58(a) does not require a separate document when the judgment or order is entered in the civil docket under Federal Rule of Civil Procedure 79(a); or

2) if Federal Rule of Civil Procedure 58(a) requires a separate document when the judgment or order is entered in the civil docket under Federal Rule of Civil Procedure 79(a) and when the earlier of these events occurs:

   (a) the judgment or order is set forth on a separate document, or

   (b) 150 days have run from the entry of the judgment or order in the civil docket under Federal Rule of Civil Procedure 79(a).

A failure to set forth a judgment or order on a separate document when required by Federal Rule of Civil Procedure 58(a) does not affect the validity of an appeal from that judgment or order.

Appeals and Review for Criminal Cases

Effect of a motion on a notice of appeal

In a criminal case, a defendant's notice of appeal must be filed in the district court within 14 days after the later of:

1) the entry of the judgment or the order being appealed; or

2) the filing of the government's notice of appeal.

When the government is entitled to appeal, its notice of appeal must be filed in the district court within 30 days after the later of:

1) the entry of the judgment or order being appealed; or

2) the filing of a notice of appeal by any defendant.

A notice of appeal filed after the court announces a decision, sentence, or order – but before the entry of the judgment or order – is treated as filed on the date of and after the entry.

If a defendant timely makes any of the following motions under the Federal Rules of Criminal Procedure, the notice of appeal from a judgment of conviction must be filed within 14 days after the entry of the order disposing of the last remaining motion or within 14 days after the entry of the judgment of conviction, whichever ends later.

The above provision applies to a timely motion:

1) for judgment of acquittal under Rule 29;

2) for a new trial under Rule 33, but is based on newly discovered evidence, only if the motion is made no later than 14 days after the entry of the judgment; or

3) for the arrest of a judgment under Rule 34.

A notice of appeal filed after the court announces a decision, sentence, or order – but before it disposes of any of the motions referred to in Rule 4(b)(3)(A) – becomes effective upon the later of the following:

1) the entry of the order disposing of the last motion; or

2) the entry of the judgment of conviction.

A valid notice of appeal is effective – without amendment – to appeal from an order disposing of motions referred to in Rule 4(b)(3)(A).

Motion for extension of time

Upon a finding of excusable neglect or good cause, the district court may – before or after the time expired, with or without motion and notice – extend the time to file a notice of appeal not to exceed 30 days from the expiration of the time otherwise prescribed by Rule 4(b).

The filing of a notice of appeal under Rule 4(b) does not divest a district court of jurisdiction to correct a sentence under Federal Rule of Criminal Procedure 35(a), nor does the filing of a motion under 35(a) affect the validity of a notice of appeal filed before entry of the order disposing of the motion.

The filing of a motion under Federal Rule of Criminal Procedure 35(a) does not suspend the time for filing a notice of appeal from a judgment of conviction.

A judgment or order is entered for purposes of this Rule 4(b) when it is entered on the criminal docket.

Appeal by an inmate confined in an institution

If an institution has a system designed for legal mail, an inmate confined must use that system to benefit from Rule 4(c)(1).

If an inmate files a notice of appeal in a civil or criminal case, the notice is timely if it is deposited in the institution's internal mail system on or before the last day for filing and:

The notice of appeal must be accompanied by:

1) a declaration in compliance with 28 U.S.C. § 1746 – or a notarized statement – setting out the date of deposit with prepaid first-class postage; or

2) evidence (such as a postmark or date stamp) showing that the notice was so deposited, and that postage was prepaid; or

The court of appeals exercises its discretion to permit the later filing of a declaration or notarized statement that satisfies Rule 4(c)(1)(A)(i).

If an inmate files the first notice of appeal in a civil case under this Rule 4(c), the 14-day period provided in Rule 4(a)(3) for another party to file a notice of appeal runs from the date when the district court dockets the first notice.

When a defendant in a criminal case files a notice of appeal under this Rule 4(c), the 30-day period for the government to file its notice of appeal runs from the entry of the judgment or order appealed from or from the district court's docketing of the defendant's notice of appeal, whichever is later.

Mistaken filing in the court of appeals

If a notice of appeal in a civil or criminal case is mistakenly filed in the court of appeals, the clerk must note on the notice the date when it was received and send it to the district clerk.

The notice is considered filed in the district court on the date noted.

Notes for active learning

Civil Procedure – Quick Facts

American courts: basic principles

1. Every state has its court system.

    Statutes enacted by the state legislature generally establish the court system's structure and the types of cases courts within a state court system may hear.

2. The Constitution provides for a **separate federal court system**.

    Article III, § 1 of the Constitution creates the **Supreme Court** and authorizes Congress to create other federal courts below the Supreme Court.

    Congress has created **federal trial courts** (i.e., federal district courts) and **intermediate appellate courts** (i.e., federal circuit courts of appeals), and a few specialized courts (e.g., U.S. Tax Court).

3. The structure of the state and federal court systems is similar.

    Like the federal system, the state courts have a set of trial courts and a state supreme court at its court system's apex.

    Many state court systems have intermediate appellate courts analogous to the federal courts of appeals (i.e., Circuit Courts).

4. Most disputes are litigated in *state courts*.

    Every state has trial courts with **broad subject matter jurisdiction**.

    Most states have several specialized (e.g., juvenile) trial courts.

5. The cases that federal courts can hear with **subject matter jurisdiction** are limited.

    The broadest categories authorized in article III § 3 are 1) cases arising under **federal law**, 2) cases between **citizens of different states**, 3) cases between **citizens and aliens**, and 4) **admiralty and maritime cases**.

6. Generally, state courts have **concurrent jurisdiction** over cases that federal courts are authorized to hear.

    For example, cases that arise under federal law usually can be brought in state court, even though general courts are authorized by Article III to hear such cases.

    If a case may be filed in either system, the **plaintiff chooses where** to file.

7. The exception to concurrent jurisdiction is that Congress, when authorizing lower federal courts to hear a particular type of case, may provide such jurisdiction is *exclusive of the states' courts*.

    It has done so for some types of cases (e.g., patent, copyright, bankruptcy).

Diversity jurisdiction

1. Article III § 2 of the Constitution authorizes federal courts to hear cases *between citizens of different states*, commonly referred to as **diversity jurisdiction**.

2. The constitutional grant in article III § 2 is satisfied as long as there is **minimal diversity** between the parties.

    Under the statutory grant, no plaintiff may be from the same state as any defendant (*Strawbridge v. Curtis*) (1806): no opposing parties may be from the same state. Thus, at least one plaintiff is from a different state than one defendant.

3. Federal district courts do not have **diversity jurisdiction** because the Constitution authorizes it. Congress must convey it by statute.

    The diversity statute, 28 U.S.C. § 1332 does not convey all diversity jurisdiction to the federal district courts.

    The diversity statute imposes an **amount in controversy requirement** (i.e., more than $75,000). The plaintiff must have a good faith belief that, if they prevail at trial, they might recover more than $75,000 (e.g., $75,000.01).

4. For individuals, federal cases hold that a person is a citizen of the state where **domiciled**.

    To establish domicile, a person must reside in a state with the *intent* to remain indefinitely.

    To be a state citizen for diversity purposes, they must be citizens of the United States (or permanent resident).

5. **Corporations are held to be state citizens** for diversity purposes.

    A corporation is a citizen of the state where 1) it is *incorporated* and 2) it has its *principal place of business*.

Arising-under jurisdiction

1. The constitutional grant *arising under* jurisdiction in Article III § 2 is liberally construed.

    If a case involves a non-frivolous federal law issue, whether raised in the original complaint or a defendant's answer, a federal court may be authorized to hear it.

2. The power of Congress to create lower federal courts includes the power to define their jurisdiction by statute.

    Article III § 2 sets the outer limit. Within the scope of Article III § 2, Congress may choose to grant federal trial courts all, some, or none of the jurisdiction authorized by the Constitution.

Thus, Congress has the power to authorize federal district courts to hear some cases that arise under federal law but not others.

3. As with diversity jurisdiction, Congress has never granted the full scope of **arising under jurisdiction** to the lower federal courts.

   In the early days of the republic, only a narrow grant of jurisdiction over claims arising under statutes, such as the patent statute, was granted.

4. Court jurisdiction is more limited than constitutional scope under 28 U.S.C. § 1331.

   Per *Mottley* (1908), a **well-pleaded complaint rule** instructs the court to refer to the *plaintiff's claim* in determining whether a case arises under federal law.

5. In most cases, the *Holmes test* (i.e., *a suit arises under the law that creates the cause of action*) determines if a case satisfies the *Mottley* requirement.

   If federal law creates the cause of action the plaintiff seeks to enforce, the federal court has jurisdiction.

   A case may arise under federal law even though the plaintiff seeks recovery on a state law claim.

   The Supreme Court has recognized that sometimes a plaintiff must establish an important federal law proposition to prove an element of a state law claim.

   A court may find that cases in this category arise under federal law so that a federal district court has jurisdiction over the case.

6. The statutes granting appellate jurisdiction to the Court are much broader than 28 U.S.C. § 1331. Consequently, many state court cases involving federal law issues may be appealed to the Supreme Court, even though the federal issue was not raised in the plaintiff's complaint so that the case could not have been filed initially in federal district court.

Removal to federal court

1. Many cases that may be brought in federal court may be filed in state court if the plaintiff prefers.

   If the plaintiff files such a case in state court, the federal removal statutes allow **defendants to remove** to federal court.

2. The standard for removal in 28 U.S.C. § 1441 allows cases to be removed to federal court **if they could have been filed originally** in federal court.

   The exception is the forum rule, which bars the removal of a diversity case **if any defendant resides in the state where the suit is brought**.

3. If a removable case is filed in state court, defendants must remove within thirty days or remain in state court.

    If a case becomes removable, the defendants have thirty days after notice.

4. **Removal is automatic**. If the defendant removes a non-removable case, it is pending in federal court once the notice of removal is filed and the state court is notified.

    Any party who believes the case was **improperly removed** or not within the federal court's subject matter jurisdiction should **move in federal court to remand** the case.

5. Motions to remand for **lack of subject matter jurisdiction** may be made **at any time before final judgment**.

    Motions for problems must be raised within thirty days of removal.

The evolution of personal jurisdiction

1. Under *Pennoyer v. Neff* (1878), which reflected nineteenth-century jurisdictional precepts, courts typically only had *in personam* (particular defendant) jurisdiction over a person if the defendant was personally served with the complaint within the forum state.

    Courts have *in rem* (*power in or about the thing*) jurisdiction over property if the property was attached before adjudicating the claim and located within the forum state.

2. *Pennoyer's* rigid doctrine was ill-equipped for an increasingly mobile society and increased interstate corporate activity.

    In *International Shoe* (1945), the court shifted its focus from the strict requirement of an in-state presence to allow jurisdiction based on a **defendant's contacts with the state.**

3. Courts have several ways to establish *in personam* jurisdiction.

    If the claim arises from the defendant's contact, a court has **specific jurisdiction** over the defendant.

    If the claim does not arise out of the defendant's contact, but the defendant has **continuous and systematic contacts with the state**, the court has general jurisdiction.

4. The Supreme Court recognizes several bases for constitutionally sufficient jurisdiction.

    A person is subject to **personal jurisdiction** where **domiciled**.

    A defendant not otherwise subject to personal jurisdiction in a state may **waive** objection or **consent to jurisdiction**.

5. A court may only exercise jurisdiction over a defendant if doing so satisfies the constitutional requirements for **personal jurisdiction**.

   The state legislature must authorize courts to exercise personal jurisdiction in the state's long-arm statute or other jurisdiction-granting statute or rule.

Long-arm statutes

1. A court can usually exercise personal jurisdiction only if: 1) a **long-arm provision authorizes it,** and 2) **constitutional.**

   "Tag" is an exception as part of a court's common law authority even when no long-arm provision authorizes it.

2. Courts often interpret the scope of the applicable long-arm statute.

Basic venue

Litigation is restricted to **convenient courts**, given the **facts** and **location of the parties.**

Relationship matrix

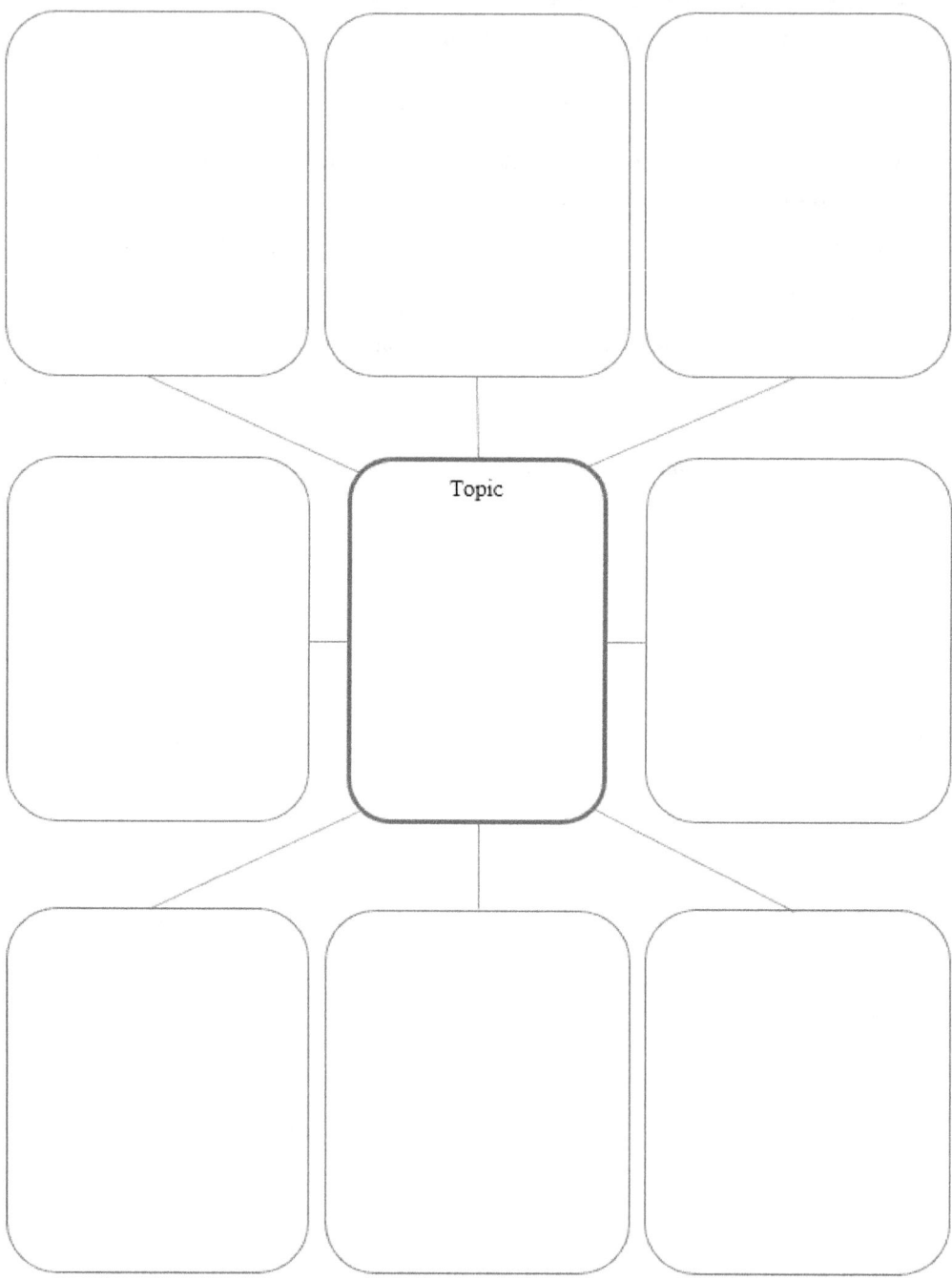

Notes for active learning

Notes for active learning

Review Questions

Multiple-choice questions

1. A Supreme Court justice who agrees with the outcome of a case, but not the reasoning, may issue a:

    A. Minority opinion
    B. Dissenting opinion
    C. Concurring opinion
    D. Non-concurring opinion

2. Federal _____ courts are appellate courts.

    A. district
    B. bankruptcy
    C. circuit
    D. equity

3. The court adhering to prior judicial decisions is known as:

    A. *res ipsa loquitur*
    B. *caveat emptor*
    C. precedents
    D. *quid pro quo*

4. Precedent requires that courts follow decisions by:

    A. higher courts within its jurisdiction
    B. the U.S. Supreme Court
    C. other appellate courts
    D. appellate courts in all jurisdictions

5. A court's resolution for a certain matter is known as a(n):

    A. *pro tempore*
    B. declaratory judgment
    C. injunction
    D. compensatory damages

6. In the federal system, trial courts are known as:

    A. District
    B. Appeals
    C. Last resort
    D. Equity

7. An appellate court does NOT:

    A. review the record of the trial court
    B. hear oral arguments from attorneys
    C. hear new evidence
    D. make legal decisions

8. Federal courts have limited jurisdiction to hear cases involving:

   A. Federal questions and diversity of citizenship
   B. Diversity of citizenship and admiralty
   C. Bankruptcy and federal crimes
   D. Diversity of citizenship and matters not subject to federal jurisdiction

9. An example of precedent is the adherence of the:

   A. appeals court to decisions of the trial court
   B. state appeals court to decisions of the Federal circuit
   C. state appeals court to decisions of the Federal District court
   D. state appeals court to decisions the U.S Supreme court

10. Under Federal Rule of Procedure, notice pleadings require:

    I. A precise statement of the claim
    II. A detailed analysis of the claim
    III. A short and plain statement of the claim

    A. I and II only
    B. II only
    C. I and III only
    D. III only

11. To request a hearing in the U.S. Supreme Court, a party files:

    A. a petition for a writ of certiorari
    B. an appeal
    C. a complaint
    D. a petition for a hearing

12. A lawsuit heard by a trial judge deciding the applicable law and facts is referred to as

    A. jury trial
    B. bench trial
    C. complex litigation
    D. appeal

13. Assume that a plaintiff files in a state trial court because they did not qualify to file in federal court. If they do not prevail at the trial court, they may appeal (assuming grounds for an appeal exist) to the:

    A. State Appeal court
    B. U.S Supreme court
    C. Federal District court
    D. Federal circuit

14. The term *en banc* means that the entire panel of judges in the:

A. U.S. Supreme court hears the case
B. appeals court hears the case
C. trial court hears the case
D. federal district court hears the case

15. To choose jurors, the judge and lawyers ask prospective jurors questions to determine if they will decide the case fairly. This process is known as:

A. *pro se*
B. *voir dire*
C. *sua sponte*
D. *ad litem*

16. Diversity of citizenship for jurisdictional purposes involves:

I. Citizens of different states
II. A citizen of a state and a citizen of a foreign country
III. A citizen and a foreign country when the foreign country is the plaintiff

A. I only
B. I and II only
C. II and III only
D. I, II and III

17. A forum-selection clause in a contract addresses:

A. Damages
B. Venue
C. Litigation
D. Liability

18. A judge's order that a party to a lawsuit refrain from doing something is a(n):

A. compensatory damages
B. declaratory judgment
C. injunction
D. *habeas corpus*

19. For a court to have authority to hear a case:

I. The plaintiff must have standing
II. The court must have jurisdiction
III. The case must be brought in the proper venue

A. I only
B. I and III only
C. III only
D. I, II and III

20. If other persons have an interest in a lawsuit, they may:

A. Consolidate
B. Intervene
C. Crosscomplain
D. Cross-reply

21. The *diversity of citizenship* to file in federal court requires that litigants are:

A. of different socio-economic backgrounds
B. of different backgrounds with an amount in controversy of $5,000
C. from different states and socio-economic backgrounds
D. from different states with an amount in controversy greater than $75,000

22. State courts have exclusive jurisdiction for:

A. Bankruptcy
B. Copyright
C. Patents
D. None of the above

23. A plurality decision means:

A. A majority cannot agree as to the outcome of the case
B. A majority decision, but not with the reasoning
C. A tie vote for the court's decision
D. None of the above

24. The complaint must:

    I. Name the parties to the lawsuit
    II. Allege the facts and law violated
    III. Contain a prayer for relief

A. I only
B. II only
C. I and II only
D. I, II and III

25. Who bears the burden of proof in a civil case?

A. The prosecution
B. The plaintiff
C. The defendant
D. The respondent

26. Depositions are taken from:

    I. Parties
    II. Witnesses
    III. Jurors

A. I only
B. I and II only
C. II and III only
D. I, II and III

27. Interrogatories are:

A. Written questions
B. Document requests
C. Medical examinations
D. Depositions

28. A motion for summary judgment asserts:

I. That the plaintiff has presented compelling evidence
II. The defendant has failed to respond to the complaint
III. There are no factual disputes to be decided

A. I only
B. II and III only
C. III only
D. I, II and III

29. All of the following are discovery devices except:

A. Depositions
B. Interrogatories
C. Production of documents
D. Cross-examination

30. Pretrial conferences are:

A. Permitted by federal and most state rules
B. Must be requested when the petition is filed
C. Formal proceedings before the court
D. None of the above

31. The term *pro se* means:

A. for a common good
B. pending a decision
C. self-representation
D. with costs

32. All of the following are pleadings EXCEPT:

A. Motion for judgment on the pleadings
B. Answer
C. Crossclaim
D. Reply

33. Trials consist of the following:

I. Jury selection
II. Opening statements
III. Jury instructions

A. I and II only
B. I and III only
C. II and III only
D. I, II and III

34. According to 28 U.S.C. § 1367(a) as the first selection of the supplemental jurisdiction statute, the federal district courts have supplemental jurisdiction for:

   A. Claims joined to a claim over which the court has original jurisdiction
   B. Claims joined to a claim over which the court has federal question or admiralty jurisdiction
   C. Claims so related to claims over which the court has original jurisdiction as those claims form part of the same case or controversy under Article III of the U.S. Constitution
   D. None of the above

35. Able, a North Carolina citizen, sues Baker in Norfolk, Virginia. Assuming federal jurisdiction, Baker may remove that case to the district court in:

   A. The federal district and division in which Norfolk is located
   B. The federal district and division in which Able lives
   C. Either of the above
   D. Neither of the above

36. A defendant has how many days to file a notice of removal in federal court after receipt of the complaint through service of process?

   A. 15 days
   B. 20 days
   C. 30 days
   D. 45 days

True/false questions

37. Cases arising under the Constitution and treaties are federal questions for jurisdiction.

   True   False

38. Decisions of limited-jurisdiction trial courts can usually be appealed to a general-jurisdiction court or appellate court.

   True   False

39. State courts have the authority to hear cases involving federal crimes.

   True   False

40. The Constitution authorizes Congress to establish inferior federal courts.

   True   False

41. The Supreme Court of the U.S. cannot come to a tie decision.

   True   False

42. If a plaintiff brings a case involving concurrent jurisdiction in state court, the defendant can remove the case to federal court.

   True   False

43. The process of bringing, maintaining, and defending a lawsuit is known as mediation.

   True   False

44. During discovery, the plaintiff alone is allowed to collect information about the case.

   True   False

45. In a lawsuit, parties are limited to evidence presented during depositions.

   True   False

46. In a civil case, the plaintiff is the petitioner if that case moves to an appellate court.

   True   False

47. The decision of a state supreme court is final.

   True   False

48. Only the defendant is allowed to file pretrial motions.

   True   False

49. The losing party in the highest state court can always appeal to the U.S. Supreme Court.

   True   False

50. There are 13 circuits in the federal court system.

   True   False

51. A majority decision is a precedent for later cases.

   True   False

52. The complaint must be served on the defendant by a sheriff.

   True   False

53. The complaint is filed by the defendant.

    True   False

54. Every state has a general jurisdiction trial court.

    True   False

55. Subject-matter jurisdiction and *in personam* jurisdiction are the same concept.

    True   False

56. If the defendant does not answer the complaint, it will be dismissed.

    True   False

57. A court could consolidate cases if several plaintiffs against the same defendant allege similar facts.

    True   False

58. Parties and witnesses can be deposed.

    True   False

59. A statute of limitations sets a period when the plaintiff must get a suit to trial.

    True   False

60. The Supreme Court accepts most of the *petitions for certiorari* filed.

    True   False

61. Less than 80% of all cases are settled before they go to trial.

    True   False

62. The commerce clause has a greater impact on business than other Constitutional provisions.

    True   False

63. The *Bill of Rights* does not apply to the actions of state governments.

    True   False

64. *Stare decisis* forms the basis of codified law.

    True   False

65. The lawyers' opening statements are not evidence, but the closing arguments are.

    True   False

66. The U.S. Supreme Court was created by the first U.S. Congress.

    True   False

67. Under a contingency fee arrangement, the lawyer receives an hourly fee.

    True   False

68. In order to be able to bring a lawsuit, the plaintiff must have standing to sue.

    True   False

69. A motion for judgment on the pleadings is based only on the pleadings.

    True   False

70. The states have *police power* to make laws promoting public health, safety, morals, and general welfare.

    True   False

71. In *United Mine Workers v. Gibbs* (1966), the Supreme Court held that when a federal court has pendent jurisdiction over a state law claim, the court must exercise that jurisdiction.

    True   False

72. Under § 1367, a court with supplemental jurisdiction over a claim must exercise that jurisdiction.

    True   False

73. Able, a Kentucky citizen, sues Baker, an Indiana citizen in state court in Indiana. The complaint is for state law negligence, and Able seeks $500,000 in damages. Baker may remove the case to federal court.

    True   False

Answer keys

1: C	11: A	21: D	31: C
2: C	12: B	22: D	32: A
3: C	13: A	23: B	33: D
4: A	14: B	24: D	34: C
5: B	15: B	25: B	35: A
6: A	16: D	26: B	36: C
7: C	17: B	27: A	
8: A	18: C	28: C	
9: D	19: D	29: D	
10: D	20: B	30: A	

37: True	51: True	65: False
38: True	52: False	66: False
39: False	53: False	67: False
40: True	54: True	68: True
41: False	55: False	69: True
42: True	56: False	70: False
43: False	57: True	71: False
44: False	58: True	72: False
45: False	59: False	73: False
46: True	60: False	
47: False	61: False	
48: False	62: True	
49: False	63: True	
50: True	64: False	

Bar Exam Information, Preparation and Test-Taking Strategies

Introduction to the Uniform Bar Examination (UBE)

Structure of the UBE

The Uniform Bar Examination (UBE) includes 1) the Multistate Bar Examination (MBE), 2) Multistate Essay Examination (MEE), and 3) Multistate Performance Test (MPT).

The MBE has 200 multiple-choice questions accounting for 50% of the UBE.

The MEE has six essays worth 30% of the UBE score.

The MPT has two legal tasks (e.g., complaint, client letter) for 20% of the UBE score.

The Multistate Bar Examination (MBE)

The Multistate Bar Examination consists of 200 four-option multiple-choice questions prepared by the National Conference of Bar Examiners (NCBE).

Of these 200 questions, 175 are scored, and 25 are unscored pretest questions.

Candidates answer 100 questions in the three-hour morning session and the remaining 100 questions in the three-hour afternoon session.

The 175 scored questions are distributed with 25 questions on each of the seven subject areas: Federal Civil Procedure, Constitutional Law, Contracts, Criminal Law and Procedure, Evidence, Real Property, and Torts.

A specified percentage of questions in each subject tests topics in those subjects.

For example, approximately one-third of Evidence questions test hearsay and its exceptions, while approximately one-third of Torts questions test negligence.

Interpreting the UBE score report

Overall score. The National Conference of Bar Examiners (NCBE) states the Uniform Bar Exam (UBE) requires a passing scaled score between 260 to 280. Scores above 280 receive a passing score in every UBE state.

The "percentile" is the number of people that scored lower. If an examinee scored in the 47th percentile, they scored higher than 47% of the examinees (and lower than 53%).

The examinee is first given a "raw score,"; based on the number of correct answers.

The raw score is adjusted by adding points to achieve the "scaled score." The number of points added is determined by a formula that compares the difficulty of the current exam to prior benchmark exams.

The comparative performance of examinees on "control questions" (prior pretest questions) given on previous exams form the basis for determining each exam's difficulty.

MBE scaled score. Examinees receive a scaled score and not an MBE "raw" score (i.e., the number of correct answers). MBE scores are scaled scores calculated by the NCBE through a statistical process used for standardized tests.

According to the NCBE, this statistical process adjusts raw scores on the current exam to account for differences in difficulty compared to previously administered exams. The scaled score is calculated from the raw score, but the NCBE does not publish the conversion formula.

Since the MBE is a scaled score, equating makes it impossible to know precisely how many questions must be answered correctly to receive a particular score. Equating allows scores from different exams to be compared since a specific scaled score represents the same level of knowledge among exams.

The MBE is curved, so just because a score is "close" to passing does not mean you are close. For example, a 124 may be in the 31st percentile and a 136 in the 62nd percentile. A 12-point difference in scaled scores equates to a 31-point percentile difference. If you are in the 120s, much preparation is needed to increase your score.

For most states, aim for a scaled score of 135 to "pass" the MBE. If you are unsure what score you need, divide the passing score by two. For example, if a 270 is needed to pass the bar, divide 268 by two to yield 135 as a threshold score on the MBE.

The importance of the MBE score

A passing MBE score depends on the jurisdiction. In jurisdictions that score on a 200-point scale, the passing score is the overall score. Passing scores are often approximately 135.

For the July 2020 bar exam, the national average MBE score was 146.1, an increase of 5 points from the July 2019 national average of 141.1.

For comparison, on the July 2018 bar, the national average MBE score was 139.5, a decrease of about 2.2 points from the July 2017 national average of 141.7.

How much the MBE contributes depends on the jurisdiction. Each jurisdiction has its policy for the relative weight given to the MBE compared to other bar exam components.

For Uniform Bar Examination (UBE) jurisdictions, the MBE component is 50%.

Most jurisdictions combine the MBE score with the state essay exam score.

The overall state candidates' performance on the MBE controls the raw state essay's conversion to scaled scores. Achieve a scaled MBE score of at least 135 to pass the bar.

MEE and MPT scores

In a UBE score report, there are six scores for the Multistate Essay Exam (MEE) and two for the Multistate Performance Test (MPT). Most states release this information.

Most states grade on a 1–6 scale (some use another scale).

In states grading on a 1–6 scale, 4 is considered a passing score.

The MEE and MPT sections are not weighted equally.

The MEE essays are worth 60%, while the MPT is 40% of the written score.

Many examinees assume that they passed the MPT and MEE portions of the exam. Examine the score report to see how you performed on these portions.

The objective of the Multistate Bar Exam

Working knowledge of the MBE objectives, the skills it tests, how it is drafted, the relationship of the parts of an MBE question, and the testing limitations provide you a substantial advantage in choosing the correct answers to MBE questions and passing the bar.

Knowing which issues are tested and the form in which they are tested makes it more manageable to learn the large body of substantive law.

The MBE's fundamental objective is to measure fairly, and efficiently which law school graduates have the necessary academic qualifications to be admitted to the bar and exceed this threshold.

The multiple-choice exam used to accomplish this objective must be of a consistent level of difficulty.

The level at which the pass decision is made must be achievable by most candidates.

The MBE tests the following skills:

- reading carefully and critically
- identifying the legal issue in a set of facts
- knowing the law that governs the legal issues tested
- distinguish between frequently confused closely-related principles
- making reasonable judgments from ambiguous facts
- understanding how limiting words make plausible-sounding choices wrong
- choosing the correct answer by intelligently eliminating incorrect choices

Notes for active learning

Preparation Strategies for the Bar Exam

An effective bar exam study plan

There are a lot of great ideas about how to prepare. Follow through with these ideas and turn them into persistent action for successful preparation.

A detailed and well-planned study schedule has benefits, such as giving you a sense of control and building confidence and proficiency.

Pick a date about 12-14 weeks before the exam (November for the February exam and April for the July exam) and use it as the start of your active study period.

Start a month earlier than many others to have a month to review as final preparation at the end.

Students have found this effective. Use an elongated prep period as a study schedule.

Most examinees prefer at least two weeks before the exam to review the material.

By planning early, you will have more time. You may want three or four final weeks to review subjects, take timed exams, and ensure that you are prepared to take the exam.

A few notes on schedule management:

> Do not *start* memorizing during your initial review period. You should be learning every week from the beginning of your study schedule. This final prep period is for reviewing and taking timed exams.

> If you stretch the study schedule over several months, plan review weeks into your schedule. For example, every four weeks, use a few days to review the governing law and take timed exams. This is a practical and fruitful approach as you will be more likely to retain the information.

Pick specific dates for specific tasks; this makes it more likely you will complete them.

Make sure the tasks are measurable. (e.g., practice two MEE essays).

Be realistic about the tasks, time, energy, and your ability to complete the items listed as tasks in preparation for the exam.

Remember to take some scheduled breaks from studying.

Exercise, sleep and take care of your physical and mental health.

If you are not in the right mental state preparing for the exam, you will likely be ineffective when studying and are less likely to pass the exam.

Focused studying

Some people are better at multiple-choice questions; others do better with essays.

The multiple-choice portion (MBE at 50%) and the essay portion (MEE at 30% and MPT at 20%) are weighted equally.

Doing poorly in one section means it will be challenging to achieve a passing score.

Identify weaknesses early in the preparation process and focus on them.

If you struggle with multiple-choice questions, dedicate extra time to practicing MBE questions.

If you struggle with writing, focus on completing MEE essays and complete MPT practice materials.

By reviewing your performance on released multiple-choice practice tests, be concerned if you consistently miss questions that are most answered correctly.

If you have problems with questions and perform below 50%, you lack the fundamental knowledge necessary to pass the MBE.

When reviewing your answers to practice questions, it is essential to review all questions and answers, even those you got right.

Make sure you got that correct answer for the right reason.

Reviewing the questions and answers is critical for success on the exam.

Spend time reviewing those basic principles and working deliberately on the straightforward (and easy) questions that supplement learning.

Advice on using outlines

As a user of this governing law book, several of the following points are moot. They are included, so you can be confident that you are using the proper resources to prep for the bar.

Having a useful governing law study guide (such as this book) is critical.

Without effective resources, it is challenging to understand, learn and apply the governing law to the facts given in the question.

Some students use outlines that make learning difficult.

A few common mistakes about outlines:

- Learning outlines that are too long (e.g., more than 100 pages per subject) or too short (e.g., a seven-page Contracts outline). You will be overwhelmed by information or never learn enough governing law.

- Spending too much time comparing several outlines for the same subject.

    For example, using different Contracts outlines and needlessly comparing them. This confusion results in an undue focus on insignificant discrepancies.

- Outlining every subject. If you are not starting to study early, this consumes too much study time. Do not attempt to outline all subjects. It may be a good idea to outline a select few problematic subjects.

Using a detailed and well-organized governing law outline (e.g., this book) is essential; it saves time, organizes concepts, reduces anxiety, and helps you score well and pass the bar.

Easy questions make the difference

Limitations on the examiners lead to the first important insight into preparation for the exam – the kind of questions that decide whether you pass.

Performance on specific questions correlates with success or failure on the bar.

By analyzing statistics, questions predicting success or failure have been identified.

In general, the most challenging questions were not particularly good predictors of failure because most people who missed them passed the bar.

However, many of the straightforward questions were excellent predictors of success.

The median raw score ranges from about 60% to 66% correct on the MBE.

The National Conference of Bar Examiners (NCBE) writes, "expert panelists reported that they believed MBE items were generally easy, correctly estimating that about 66% of candidates would select the right answer to a typical item."

Depending on the exam's difficulty, in most states, scoring slightly below the median (miss up to 80 questions) still passes.

The most important questions to determine if you pass are not the exceedingly challenging ones but the easy ones where 90% of the examinees answer correctly.

The easy questions usually test a basic and regularly tested point of substantive law.

The wrong choices (i.e., the distracters) are typically easy to eliminate.

Your first task in preparing for the MBE is to get easy questions correct.

Study plan based upon statistics

These statistics show that an excellent performance on either the MBE questions (approximately 67% correct) or the state essays (4s on essays) assures you a passing score.

If you fail the MBE by 9 points or the essays by 5 points, the probability of passing the bar is in the single digits.

Put effort into performing well on the MBE questions for the following reasons.

- The questions are objective, and there are enough questions that are predictable concerning content and structure that it is possible, through reasonable effort, to answer 67% of the questions correctly.

- Studying the MBE first has the added advantage of preparing the necessary substantive law for state essays.

- The essays cover several subjects, the precise topic tested is unpredictable, and the answers are graded subjectively by graders who work quickly.

You had three years of law school practice with essays and less experience with multiple-choice questions.

Master the MBE before spending time preparing for the essays.

Factors associated with passing the bar

Based on an analysis of statistics from students' performance, the following factors predict the likelihood of passing the bar:

LSAT score

First-year Grade Point Average (GPA)

LSAT scores are a significant predictor of success on the bar because the LSAT requires similar multiple-choice test-taking skills as the MBE.

The LSAT tests many of the types of legal reasoning tested on the MBE.

A lower LSAT can be overcome by a comprehensive study of the MBE governing law, but these students must work harder.

Most of the subjects tested (e.g., constitutional law, civil procedure, contracts, criminal law, real property, torts) on the MBE are taken in the first year of law school.

First-year GPA measures mastery of subjects, preparedness for exams, and the ability to understand legal principles and apply them to given fact patterns.

The MBE measures the same factors but in a multiple-choice format instead of essays.

Pass rates based on GPA and LSAT scores

Past statistics indicate that law students with LSAT scores above 155 and a first-year GPA above 3.0 are reasonably assured of passing the bar.

They should study conscientiously and take practice MBEs to perform at the level needed, but they have little cause to panic.

Students with LSAT scores between 150 and 155 and a first-year GPA between 2.5 and 3.0 are in a bit more danger of failing and need to undertake rigorous preparation.

They must achieve a scaled score of 135 and take released practice exams and understand the reasons for incorrect choices. They should prepare for state essays by learning the governing laws in this book.

Students with LSAT scores between 145 and 150 and a first-year GPA between 2.2 and 2.5 have a moderate chance of passing the bar from deliberate efforts.

These students should not rely on ordinary commercial bar reviews and need intense training, particularly on the MBE component of the bar. They must devote 50-60 hours per week for seven weeks to prepare for the bar by learning the format and content of substantive law tested on the MBE. They should take released practice exams under exam conditions and conscientiously study the questions missed.

Students with LSAT scores below 145 and a GPA below 2.2 have had a failure rate of approximately 80%.

They must prep faithfully and conscientiously beyond the advice above and must engage in a rigorous course of study, more than is demanded by a traditional bar review course.

Notes for active learning

Learning and Applying the Substantive Law

Knowledge of substantive law

The fundamental reason for missing a question is 1) a failure to know the principle of law controlling the answer or 2) failure to understand how that principle is applied.

You must know and apply the governing law to pass the bar. If you do not know the governing law, you will not apply it to answer correctly.

Many students *think* they understand the governing law but do not know the nuances. Do not assume that you understand the governing (i.e., substantive) law. It is prevalent for students not to know the governing law well.

Re-learn the substantive and procedural law taught in first-year courses.

A major mistake is not to memorize the governing law outlined in this book.

The multiple-choice and essay portions test nuances and details of governing law. It is essential to analyze the governing law as it is applied in the context of the question.

On the multiple-choice section, many questions require fine-line distinctions between similar principles of law.

Several multiple-choice answers will *seem* correct, given the limited time to answer. If your knowledge of the governing law is suboptimal, you will not make these subtle distinctions and will have to guess on many questions.

For the essay to be developed, you must know the governing law and apply it to the issues within the call of the question.

If you do not know the governing law, you will not state the correct rule in your essay. You will be unable to apply the correct rule to the fact pattern.

Where to find the law

The questions must be related to the subject matter outlined in the bar examiners' (NCBE) materials.

While the NCBE outline is broad and ambiguous, years of experience with the exam delineate the scope of material you must learn.

The governing law covered in this book is foundational to the exam. The governing law statements were compiled by analyzing questions released by the multistate examiners. The analysis revealed a limited number of legal principles repeatedly tested.

Review these principles before taking practice exams and understand how they are applied to obtain the correct answer.

The property questions are probably the most difficult. The fact patterns are usually long and involve many parties in complex transactions.

In preparing for the exam, learn basic property principles and apply them. However, extensive studying into property law's crevices is not necessary to score well on these questions.

Feel confident that you do not have to go beyond the information provided in this book to find the governing law.

Controlling authority

The examiners have specified the sources of authority for the correct answers.

In Constitutional Law and Criminal Procedure, it is Supreme Court decisions.

In Criminal Law, it is common law.

In Evidence, the Federal Rules of Evidence controls.

In Torts and Property, it is the generally accepted view of United States law.

The UCC is the controlling authority in sales (Article 2) questions.

The NCBE released questions, and the published answers determine the controlling law through deduction.

Recent changes in the law

The exam is prepared months before it is given because of logistical requirements. Therefore, the examiners cannot incorporate recent changes in the law into the questions.

Recent changes in the law will not form the basis for correct answers.

If a recent change makes an answer initially designated as the correct answer to be incorrect, the examiners will credit more than one answer.

The recent holding of a Supreme Court case will not be tested for about two years since the decision was published.

Lesser-known issues and unusual applications

Some of the challenging exam questions are based on obscure principles of law.

Missing the most challenging questions will not cause you to fail the exam if you have a solid understanding of the governing law. You can learn these principles and answer the question correctly, thereby improving your overall performance.

There are instances where the correct answers are different from the usual rules.

For example, hearsay evidence inadmissible at trial is admissible before a judge hearing evidence on a preliminary question of fact (e.g., Federal Rules of Evidence 104(a)).

Practice applying the governing law

Some students know the governing law but have problems *applying* it to the facts.

The exam is as much about testing skills as it is about testing the governing law.

Therefore, knowledge of the governing law is not enough to pass.

You must practice answering multiple-choice questions and writing well-organized, coherent, and complete essays where you apply the governing law to the given facts.

Know which governing law is being tested

A typical wrong answer (i.e., distracter) on a question is an answer which is correct under a body of law other than the governing law being tested.

An example is a question governed by Article 2 of the Uniform Commercial Code (UCC), where an offer is irrevocable if:

1) it is in writing,

2) made by a merchant, and

3) states that it is irrevocable.

One of the wrong answers states the correct rule under the common law of contracts, where an offer is revocable unless consideration is paid (i.e., an option) for the promise to keep it open.

Answers which are always wrong

Some commonly used distracters are always wrong and can be eliminated quickly.

For example, a choice in an evidence question says, "character can only be attacked by reputation evidence." This choice is wrong because both opinion and reputation evidence is admissible under the Federal Rules of Evidence when character attacks are permissible.

Honing Reading Skills

Reading skills are critical. The basic level is reading to understand the facts, identify the issue and keep the parties distinct. A mistake at this juncture results in answering incorrectly, no matter how much law is known.

Understanding complex transactions

If the question involves a transaction with many parties, diagram the transaction before analyzing the choices.

The diagram should show the relationship between the parties (e.g., grantor-grantee, assignor-assignee), the transaction date, and the person's relationships in the transaction (e.g., donee, *bona fide* purchaser).

Impediments to careful reading

Two reasons candidates fail to read carefully are:

1) hurrying through a question,

2) fatigue due to a lack of sleep or strain caused by the exam.

A careful test taker maintains a steady, deliberate pace during the exam. Practice in advance and be well-rested on the test day.

Reading too much into a question

The examiners are committed to designing questions, which are "a fair index of whether the applicant has the ability to practice law." Psychometric experts ensure that they are fair and unbiased.

Even though you must read every word of these carefully drafted questions, do not read the question to find some bizarre interpretation.

The examiners must ask fair questions and not rely on "tricks." Reading too much into a question and looking for a trick lurking behind every fact leads to the wrong answer often.

It is the straightforward questions that determine whether you pass, not the occasional challenging question that tests some arcane principle of law.

Therefore, take questions at face value.

Read the call of the question first

Before reading the facts, read the call of the question because it indicates the task for selecting the correct answer. This perspective focuses your attention before reading the facts.

The question contains many *words of art*, such as "most likely," "best defense," or "least likely," which govern the correct answer.

The call is often phrased positively; the "best argument" or "most likely result."

Read answers for consistency with the question and eliminate inconsistent choices.

Negative calls

When the call of the question is negative, asking for the "weakest argument" or asking which of the options is "not" in a specified category, examine each option with the perspective that the choice with those negative characteristics is the correct answer.

After reading and understanding the question stem, read the call of the question again before reading the choices.

Analyze each choice with the requirements specified in the call of the question.

Read all choices

Never pick an answer until carefully reading all the choices. The objective is to pick the best answer, which cannot be determined until comparing the choices.

Sometimes the difference between the right and wrong answer is that one choice is more detailed or precisely sets forth the applicable law. You do not know that until reading all the answers carefully.

Broad statements of black letter law may be correct

When reading an answer, do not rule out choices with imprecise statements of the applicable *black letter* law.

If the examiners always included a choice that was precisely on point, the questions would be too easy. Instead, they often disguise the wording used in the correct answer.

For example, the Federal Rules of Evidence contain an elaborate set of relevancy rules that limit the right to introduce evidence of repairs after an accident. If there was a question where the introduction of that evidence was permissible, and no choices specifically cite the exception to the general rule of exclusion, an answer phrased with the general rule of relevancy "Admissible because its probative value outweighs its prejudicial effect," would be the correct answer.

Multiple-Choice Test-Taking Tactics

Determine the single correct answer

Increase the odds of picking the correct answer based on technical factors independent of substantive (governing) law knowledge.

The examiners' limitation is that every question must have one demonstrably correct and three demonstrably incorrect answers, limiting how the examiners write the choices.

From the question's construction, this limitation may give clues about the answer.

Process of elimination

Answering a multiple-choice question is not finding the ideal answer to the question asked but instead picking the best option.

Eliminate choices and evaluate the remaining choice for plausibility.

Eliminate choices that state an incorrect proposition of law or do not relate to the facts.

If you eliminate three options and the remaining one is acceptable, pick it and move on.

Elimination increases the odds

It takes about 125 correct answers to pass the MBE. An important strategy in reaching that number is intelligently eliminating choices.

If you are sure of the answer to only 50 of the 200 questions on the exam and confidently eliminate two of the four choices on the remaining 150 questions. Guess between the two remaining choices, and the odds predict 75 correct.

Those 75 correct, coupled with 50 questions you were confident of the answer, produce a raw score of 125 on the MBE and a scaled score above the benchmark 135.

Unfortunately, you cannot avoid guessing on questions, but intelligent methods reduce options to only two viable choices.

Sometimes you might not be able to eliminate the wrong answers just because you are sure of the answer to one of the choices. Eliminating with confidence even one choice increases the probability of correctly answering the question.

Eliminating two wrong answers

Specific questions on the MBE are challenging because of distinguishing between two choices when selecting the best answer.

A typical comment from examinees leaving the exam is, "I could not decide between the last two choices."

The positive side of that problem is eliminating two of the four choices.

Pick the winning side

The most common choice pattern is the "two-two" pattern – two choices state that the plaintiff prevails, and two that the defendant prevails.

The best approach for this type of question is to rely on your knowledge of the law or instinctive feeling to which conclusion is correct.

In a question with two choices on one side and two on the other side of a court's decision, first, pick a choice on the side you think should prevail.

Distinguish between the explanations following this conclusion and pick the choice that best justifies it.

Distance between choices on the other side

If the justifications following the conclusion for the side you chose seem indistinguishable, look at the explanations for the choices on the other side.

If the reasons for the choices on the other side are readily distinguishable, and one appears reasonable and the other incorrect, reconsider your initial conclusion.

Remember, the examiner is required to provide a distinguishable reason why one explanation of a general conclusion is correct, and the other is wrong.

That obligation does not exist if the general conclusion itself is incorrect.

Suppose choices (A) and (B) on one side look correct; that is, they are reasonable and consistent with the fact pattern. One of the choices with the opposite conclusion, answer (C), seems incorrect or inconsistent with the facts, and answer (D) with the same general conclusion sounds reasonable. From a strictly technical viewpoint, the best choice is answer (D).

Questions based upon a common fact pattern

There are several instances where two or more questions are based on the same facts.

Look at the second question's wording to guide the first question's correct answer. When asked to assume an answer to a first question from a fact pattern to answer the second question, the probability is high that the answer to the first question follows that assumption.

For example, if the first question has two choices beginning with "P prevails" and two with "D prevails," and the second question starts with "If P prevails," it is likely one of the "P prevails" choices is correct for the first question. If you picked "D prevails," think carefully before selecting it as the final answer.

Multiple true/false issues

In addition to true/false questions, the exam sometimes states three propositions in the root of the question and tests characteristics of those propositions in the call of the question.

The choices list various combinations of propositions.

The difference between this type of question and the double true/false question is that only four of the eight possible combinations fit into the options. It is possible to answer correctly even if you are not sure of all propositions' truth or falsity but are sure of one.

Correctly stated, but the inapplicable principle of law

The task of the examiners is to make the wrong choices look attractive. A creative way to accomplish this is to write a choice that impeccably states a rule of law that is not applicable because of facts in the root of the question.

For example, in a question where a person is an assignee, not a sublessee, one of the choices may correctly state the law for sublessees, but it is inapplicable to the fact pattern.

Therefore, these answer choices with inapplicable law can be confidently eliminated.

"Because" questions

Conjunctions are commonly used in the answers. It is essential to understand their role in determining whether a choice is correct.

The word "because" connects a conclusion and the reason for that conclusion with the facts in the body of the question.

There are two requirements for a question using "because" to be correct:

1) the conclusion must be correct,

2) the reasoning must logically follow based upon facts in the question, and the statement which follows "because" must be legally correct.

If the "because" choice has the correct result for the wrong reason, it is incorrect.

"If" questions

The conjunction "if" requires a much narrower focus than "because."

When a choice contains an "if," determine whether the entire statement is true, assuming that the proposition which follows the "if" is true.

There is no requirement that facts in the root of the question support the proposition following "if." There is no requirement for facts in the question to support the proposition that such a construction be reasonable.

"Because" or "if" need not be exclusive

There is no requirement for the conclusion following "if" or "because" to be exclusive.

For example, if a master could be liable in tort under the doctrine of *respondeat superior* or because the master was *negligent*, a choice using "if" or "because" holding the master liable would be correct if it stated either reason, even though the master might be liable for the other reason.

Exam tip for "because"

Notice that in an answer that would have been correct, the word "because" limits the facts you could consider to those in the body of the question containing specific facts.

The difference between the effect of "if" and "because" controls the answer.

Identify those limited situations (e.g., where the appropriate standard is strict liability) and distinguish them from those that are satisfactory (e.g., if the standard is negligence).

"Only if" requires exclusivity

Sometimes the words "only if" are used to distinguish between the two "affirmed" choices to make one wrong.

When an option uses the words "only if," assume that the entire proposition is correct as long as the words following "only if" are true.

The critical difference, where "only if" is used, is that the proposition cannot be true except when the condition is true. If there is another reason for the same result to be reached, the choice is wrong.

"Unless" questions

The conjunction "unless" has the same function as "only if," except that it precedes a negative exclusive condition instead of a positive exclusive condition.

It is essentially the mirror image of an "only if" choice.

For an option using "unless," reverse and substitute the words "only if" for "unless."

Limiting words

Choices can be made incorrect with limiting words that require that a proposition be true in all circumstances or under no circumstances.

Examples of limiting words include *all*, *any*, *never*, *always*, *only*, *every*, and *plenary*.

Notes for active learning

Making Correct Judgment Calls

Applying the law to the facts

Most questions give a fact pattern and ask which choice draws the correct legal conclusion required by the call of the question.

The first skill required is to draw inferences from facts given to place the conduct described in the question in the appropriate legal category.

The second skill is to apply the appropriate legal rule to conduct in that category and choose the option which reaches the appropriate conclusion.

The process of drawing inferences from a fact pattern and placing conduct in an appropriate category often requires judgment.

Bad judgment equals the wrong answer

To make the questions difficult, the examiners often place the conduct near the border of two different legal classifications.

Decide which side of the demarcation the conduct falls on. Inevitably, reasonable people can differ on these judgments.

If your judgment does not match the examiners, you will likely answer the question incorrectly, no matter how much law you know.

Mitigate this problem by reviewing released questions involving judgment calls where the examiners have published correct answers (i.e., their judgment call).

For example, a death occurring because the parties played Russian roulette is considered *depraved heart murder*, not *involuntary manslaughter*.

Judgment calls happen

Difficult judgment calls occur several times on the exam, and you are likely to make some close judgment calls incorrectly.

While this adds to the frustrations of multiple-choice tests, it is part of the exam.

By narrowing judgment call questions to two choices and guessing, you will get approximately half of them correct.

You will not fail the exam solely because you were unlucky on judgment calls.

The examiners remove many judgment calls by procedural devices.

The importance of procedure

The question may not ask what a jury should find on the facts.

The answer may be controlled by the procedural context of the criminal prosecution.

For example, it is given that the jury has found the defendant guilty of murder, and the only question on appeal is whether the judge should have granted a motion to dismiss at the end of hearing evidence. This is because a reasonable jury looking at the facts and inferences most favorable to the prosecution should not have found the defendant guilty of murder.

The same procedural issues exist when the question asks if a motion for summary judgment should be allowed or if the court should direct a verdict.

Exam Tips and Suggestions

Timing is everything

The time given to complete the exam is usually adequate if you practiced enough questions to improve speed and efficiency to the required level.

As you get closer to the test date, just doing practice questions is not enough.

You need to time your practice. Take previously released exams in two three-hour periods on the same day. Since these practice exams are approximately the same length as the exam, you will know if you have a timing problem.

If you do not practice under timed conditions, you risk exhausting time on the exam before answering all the questions.

Practice your timing under test-like conditions to know if the timing will be an issue. If you cannot complete the practice exam, you will have trouble with the exam.

If time is an issue, adjust your pace and continue practicing.

All questions do not require the same amount of time.

An approach for when time is not an issue

If you can complete 100 questions in three hours, use this strategy. At the start of the exam, break the allotted time into 15-minute intervals and write them down.

Set an initial pace of 9 questions every fifteen minutes.

Check your progress at each 15-minute interval.

If you completed 18 questions in the first half-hour, 36 in the first hour, 72 in the first two hours, and 90 in the first two and a half hours, you are on target to complete the exam on time. At this pace, you should complete 100 questions in two hours and forty-six minutes.

This leaves 14 minutes to check the answer sheet, revisit troublesome questions, or use the time to go a little slower on the last questions when fatigue impairs acuity.

If you find that your careful pace is faster than the budgeted 9 questions every 15 minutes, work at a faster pace, but use the extra time on the more challenging questions or in rechecking your work at the end.

Do *not* change the original answer choice unless you have a specific reason.

It is unwise to leave the exam early.

An approach for when time is an issue

During practice, continue answering questions to complete the section even after the time for self-paced exams has expired. Note which question you completed within the allocated time. Strive to complete the questions within the allotted time during your final exam prep.

If you learn from taking the practice test that you may not finish the questions in the allotted time on the actual exam, skip those questions with a long fact pattern followed by only one question. Keep your place on the answer sheet by skipping the row.

Return to those questions at the end and complete as many as time permits. Before turning your exam in, guess at the rest to reduce the number of random guesses.

Answer every question, even if you have not read the question, since wrong answers do *not* count against you.

Difficult questions

If you do not know the answer, do not spend a disproportionate amount of time on it since each question counts the same. Mark it in the test booklet, make a shrewd guess within the budgeted time and come back if time allows.

Do *not* leave questions unanswered. No points are deducted for wrong answers.

Minimize fatigue to maximize your score

The mental energy required to answer all the multiple-choice questions under stress produces fatigue (even with a lunch break).

Fatigue slows processing questions effectively and impairs reading comprehension. You may process questions more slowly at the end of each session and more quickly at the beginning before fatigue sets in.

Take at least two released exams under timed conditions to know how significantly fatigue affects your performance.

Be sure to arrive at the exam site on time. If necessary, stay at a nearby hotel rather than getting up early and risking a long drive the morning of the exam.

Relax during the lunch break and do not discuss the morning session with others.

You should know enough about your metabolism to eat the correct foods during the exam and reinforce appropriate caffeine levels if appropriate.

Proofread the answer sheet

As you decide on each correct answer, circle the corresponding letter in the exam book, and mark the appropriate block on the answer sheet.

The answer sheet is the only document graded by the examiners.

At the pace of 9 questions per 15 minutes, about 14 minutes should remain. Spend that time proofreading the answer sheet. Verify the answers circled to be certain that you marked the appropriate block on the answers.

Ensure that there are no blanks, and no questions have two answers.

Do *not* use this time to change an answer already selected unless you have a particularly good reason to change it.

If you have erased, ensure the erasure is thorough, or the computer may reject the answer because it cannot distinguish between marked answers.

If you have time after proofreading, review the problematic questions, and re-think the answers chosen. However, even after careful thought, hesitate to change an answer.

Do not leave any section of the exam early; use the allotted time wisely.

Intelligent preparation over a sustained period

There is no easy way to conquer an exam as challenging and comprehensive as the MBE, except through practice and an investment of time and effort well before the exam.

By diligently preparing, practicing questions, and intelligently assessing why questions were answered incorrectly, your skills for the exam will improve substantially.

Continue to improve those skills by following the advice given herein until reaching a proficiency level enabling you to pass the bar. This proficiency is accurately measured in multiple-choice format questions.

Some students will have to work harder to achieve the required proficiency.

The tools are in this study guide, and any law school graduate can be successful in passing the bar if they invest the required time and effort to be prepared.

Notes for active learning

Essay Preparation Strategies and Essay-Writing Suggestions

Memorize the law

Do not make the mistake of waiting too long before memorizing the governing law. Start learning the governing law early to be better prepared and pass the exam.

Memorize essential principles and focus on highly tested governing law.

Focus on the highly tested essay rules

Do not treat all subjects the same when you prepare for the essay portion of the exam.

Some governing law topics are tested more than others. It is crucial to focus on the highly tested topics (e.g., torts, contracts. property, civil procedure).

Know and apply enough governing laws to pass the bar – focus on commonly tested governing laws (e.g., negligence) provided in this book.

Practice writing essay answers each week

Practicing is crucial to a high score on essays. Practice regularly and avoid procrastination for this essential component of bar prep.

Incorporate practicing essay writing into your exam study schedule. To reduce procrastination, schedule time for writing practice essays each week.

For the MPT, practice by drafting full MPTs. Most examinees procrastinate on preparing for the MPT; there is nothing to memorize.

Do not make the *fatal mistake* of not practicing. The MPT portion is worth 20% of the UBE score.

Know the format and *practice that format to* increase your UBE score. This practice will increase your score and the probability of passing the bar.

Add one essay-specific subject each week

The Multistate Essay Exam (MEE) subjects include the 7 MBE subjects plus the 5 subjects of Business Associations (Agency, Partnerships, Corporations, and LLCs), Conflict of Laws, Family Law, Trusts and Estates, and Secured Transactions (UCC Article 9).

Combine highly tested subjects (e.g., torts) with less-tested subjects (e.g., secured transactions) and complex topics (e.g., contracts) with easier topics (e.g., business associations).

From preparation, know which subjects you struggle with and require a focused effort to master the essential governing law.

Make it easy for the grader to award points

Your answer to a question will probably be read in less than five minutes by a grader with a checklist to find that you have seen the issues and discussed them intelligently. Writing organized and clear answers makes it easy for the essay grader to award points.

Use headings for each of the major issues.

If the question suggests a structure for the answer because it is divided into parts or because the facts present a series of discrete issues, use the structure of the question, which is probably the structure of the checklist.

Use the IRAC method for the essay questions: state the issue, state the Rule. Apply the rule to the facts and conclude. IRAC seems simple, but following this approach makes it easier for the grader to know that you identified and addressed every issue and applied the law to the facts given.

IRAC results in more points during the exam.

Do not spend time trying to formulate eloquent issue statements. The question often outlines the issues, so an eloquent issue statement is redundant, and issue statements do not earn extra points.

Many examinees spend too much time developing an impressive issue statement and omit other essentials of their analysis (e.g., truncated analysis section).

An issue statement "Torts" or "Is the defendant liable for negligence?" is enough.

Do not waste time arguing both sides. There are no "two sides" for many essays to argue on bar essays because these are not law school essays.

Apply the law to facts and conclude unless asserting each party has good arguments.

Conclusion for each essay question

Points will be lost unless you conclude for each issue identified in the facts or are asked to address it in the call of the question.

Use caution starting the essay with the conclusion unless confident it is correct.

Many sample answers provided by the National Conference of Bar Examiners start with a definite and strong conclusion. Use caution to start with a conclusion unless confident (e.g., NCBE sample responses) your conclusion is correct.

Starting with a conclusion that is not correct draws attention to an incorrect conclusion at the start, which may influence the grader disproportionality. The grader may lose faith in your answer from the onset, and it is advisable to have a neutral heading rather than a firm conclusion that is wrong.

Tips for an easy-to-read essay

Use paragraph breaks between the Issue, Rule, Analysis, and Conclusion. Paragraph break makes it easy for the grader to read and score your essays. Additionally, this approach makes the answer appear longer and more complete.

Emphasize keywords and phrases. Underline key phrases so the grader notices that you addressed the governing law and applied it to the facts given.

After graders score several essays on the same topic, they scan essays for specific phrases that they expect to locate within a complete essay.

Think before you write

Read each question carefully to understand the facts and their necessary implications thoroughly and accurately.

After skimming the question, spend time on the focus line at the end of the question. Review the facts with the call of the question in mental focus.

Write a short outline of the issues raised. Outline in your mind the issues; state to yourself the tentative conclusions; test each conclusion from the standpoints of law and common sense; revise, as necessary.

Decide on a logical, orderly, and convincing arrangement for the response. Until then, you are not ready to write the answer.

Of the thirty-six minutes allotted to each essay, spend 15 minutes on issue spotting and organization and about twenty minutes writing the answer.

The ability to think and communicate like a lawyer

The Board knows that you have completed law school, under competent instructors, and have passed law school exams. The bar does not challenge the results of your law school courses.

The exam tests the ability to apply what you have learned to facts that might arise in practice and which, in some instances, involve several fields of law. The value of an answer depends not only on the correctness of the conclusions but on displaying essential legal principles and thinking like a lawyer.

Conclude on each issue presented. If a conclusion is derived from fuzzy facts, construct a well-reasoned argument supporting your conclusion to receive full credit regardless of if you conclude the same as the examiners.

If the correct answer depends on a provision of substantive law, which you are not familiar with, you can obtain a passing answer to the question by reaching a well-reasoned conclusion applying general law principles.

Do not try to limit the question to a particular subject area. Many questions combine traditional subjects, and you must be prepared to answer the question applying principles you learned across various subjects.

Do not restate the facts

The examiners know the facts; there is no time to waste. Do not restate the facts but use them to apply and integrate legal principles in writing the essay.

Do not fight the facts, particularly the focus line of the question.

For example, if the facts state that A executed a valid will, write about valid wills. If the question asks you to argue on behalf of A, do not argue on behalf of B because B has a prevailing argument. However, raise potential arguments which could be made on behalf of B and counter them in arguing on behalf of A.

Do not state abstract or irrelevant propositions of law

It is usually undesirable to begin an answer with a legal proposition. If the proposition is applicable, it will be more appropriate later to indicate the reason for your conclusion. If it is not applicable, do not state a surplus fact or legal principle.

Although it is seldom necessary to state an applicable rule of law in detail, make a sufficient reference to it so that the examiner appreciates your knowledge of the principle and conditions when it applies.

Do not, by speculating on different facts, nor in other ways, work into your answer some point of law with which you happen to be familiar, but which does not apply to the answer. Importantly, the examiners are not interested in knowing how many rules of law you know, but your ability to apply the applicable rules to the facts.

If the question says that A and B in the above hypothetical are unrelated, do not talk about the results which would occur if they were husband and wife.

Use the principles of law applicable to the call of the question and the facts. You must state the principles of applicable law to demonstrate to the examiner that you know the elements of the rule and how they apply to these facts.

For example, if the facts said that A transferred to B (a non-relative) the money necessary for B to purchase Blackacre from C and asks who owns Blackacre, you would say, "Since A furnished the consideration for the purchase of Blackacre and B took the title to the property in their name, B holds title to Blackacre in a resulting trust for A.

Do not detail the black letter law of resulting trusts since you have shown your knowledge by properly applying the facts to the law of resulting trusts.

Do not fight the facts and address a contrary fact not presented. The examiners may take points away if you make that mistake because you are not focused on the issues presented.

Discuss all the issues raised

A grasp of all the issues is essential.

For example, if there are three issues in a question, a discussion of only one issue, no matter how masterly, if coupled with omitting the others, could not result in 100% credit. It would probably result in a score of 33%.

The exam includes many issues in most questions so it can be graded mechanically. This maintains consistency across a group of several graders for each exam question.

The grader has a checklist of issues and awards most points for the examinee that identifies issues and intelligently discusses each.

Failure to see and discuss enough issues intelligently is probably the biggest reason for failure on the essay portion of the exam.

Methods for finding all issues

Use all the facts presented. Failure to discuss facts probably means that you missed important issues.

If you must decide in the early part of the question (e.g., does the court have jurisdiction) and you decide that issue so the remaining facts become irrelevant, make an alternative assumption ("If the court does have jurisdiction") and answer the question in the alternative using facts which would otherwise be irrelevant.

Do not avoid issues because you are not sure of the substantive law. If the examiners stated that X's nephew helped X escape after a crime, discuss the nephew's status as an accessory after the fact. If you do not know whether he is a close enough relative to be exempt under the statute, answer this issue by making alternative assumptions.

Indicators requiring alternative arguments

Ambiguous terms – if there are words in the fact pattern that are neutral or ambiguous such as "put up," the examiners look for possible interpretations of these terms.

Language in quotes – language placed in quotes is almost always ambiguous and must be construed as part of the answer.

Avoid ambiguous, rambling statements and verbosity

Generally, do not use compound sentences. Two separate sentences are preferred.

Complex sentences are particularly useful to apply the facts of the question to the applicable principle of law.

For example, in the previous resulting trust hypothetical, write, "Since B purchased Blackacre and took title in their name with money furnished by A, A holds title to Blackacre in a resulting trust, even if B has not signed a memorandum."

Avoid undue repetition

If the same principle of law and conclusion apply to two parts of an answer, state it once in detail, and refer back for the second part.

For example, if you have discussed A's liability and now must discuss B's liability, say, "B is also guilty of murder for the same reasons as A. (see discussion above)."

Avoid slang and colloquialism

The examiners judge your formal writing style.

If the examiner shows humor with names and events, do not show your sense of humor.

> Use the standard abbreviations:
>
> P for Plaintiff
>
> D for Defendant
>
> K for Contract
>
> BFP for *Bona Fide* purchaser

Write legibly and coherently

Printing is usually easier to read than handwriting.

Use all the pages, and do not crowd your answer.

Plan your answer so that you do not have to use inserts and arrows.

Timing strategies

On the MEE, you must complete six equally weighted essay questions in three hours; an average of 30 minutes per question.

You have flexibility with time limitations as questions are not of the same difficulty.

There are two absolute figures:

>spend no more than 45 minutes on any question,

>spend at least 20 minutes on each question.

Be careful about not going over the time limit on the first question because this will require a readjustment of your timing for the entire session. If you miss the deadlines, re-divide your remaining time so that you will have an equal amount of time on each question.

If you go over by 15 minutes a question, do not allocate 30 minutes for other questions.

Stay focused

Do not start by reading the entire exam. Answer the questions in order and do not consider more than one question at a time.

After answering, put it out of your mind and not worry about your response. Keep your mind clear to focus on the next question.

Proofread your answers as time permits.

Law school essay grading matrix

An "A" answer is an outstanding response. It correctly and fully identifies dispositive issues and sub-issues raised by the question. The answer states the applicable legal rules and sub-rules with precision. It analyzes the question thoroughly with the applicable rules and explores alternative analysis where appropriate. It applies the law to the facts to conclude and is not cluttered by irrelevant matters. An "A" answer demonstrates an objectively superior mastering of the subject. An answer is not an "A" answer simply because it is better than most students' answers.

A "B" answer is a good response. It presents the four components of a good answer (issues, rules, analysis & application, and conclusion), but it does so in a way that could be improved. For example, it may be that not all critical issues have been spotted, or the issues are not presented clearly. The statement of legal rules captures that basic law but may not develop the law's complexities or nuances. The analysis is competent but lacks subtlety and may be somewhat simplistic or conclusory.

A "C" answer is a minimally competent response. It contains the four components of a good answer (issues, rules, analysis & application, and conclusion) but may not distinguish them. Perhaps only some issues have been identified while others are missed. The rules of law lack completeness or accuracy. The analysis and application may be shallow and conclusory. Conclusions may be questionable and not well-defended.

A "D" answer lacks basic components. It may identify the wrong issues or none. Rules are stated incorrectly. The analysis is conclusory or absent. The law is not applied to the facts coherently. Conclusions are unsupported or missing. The response exhibits a lack of knowledge of legal issues and rules or demonstrates an inability to engage in legal analysis.

Best wishes with your preparation!

Appendix

STERLING
Test Prep

Overview of American Law

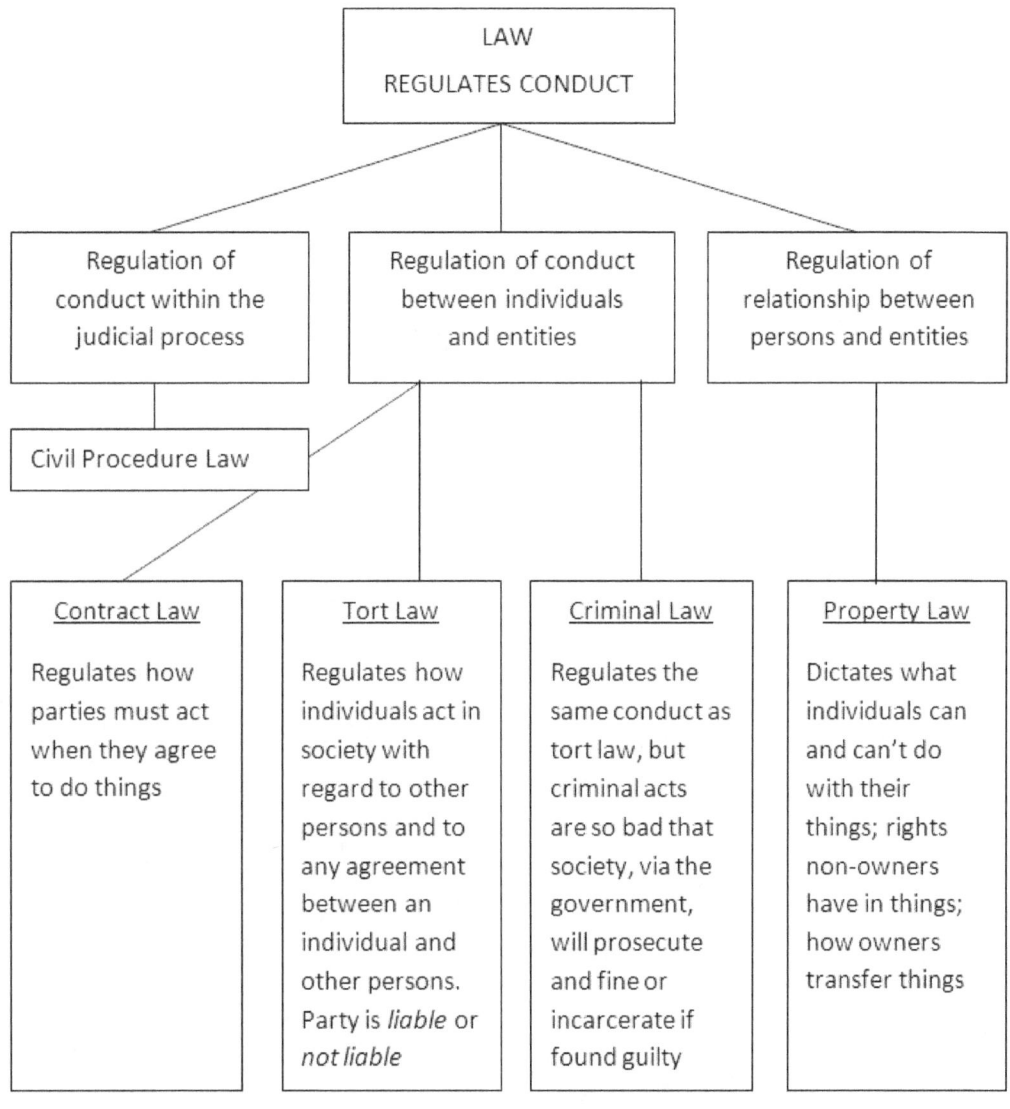

U.S. Court Systems – Federal and State Courts

There are two kinds of courts in the USA – federal courts and state courts.

Federal courts are established under the U.S. Constitution by Congress to decide disputes involving the Constitution and laws passed by Congress. A state establishes state and local courts (within states, local courts are established by cities, counties, and other municipalities).

Jurisdiction of federal and state courts

The differences between federal courts and state courts are defined by jurisdiction.[1] Jurisdiction refers to the kinds of cases that a particular court is authorized to hear and adjudicate (i.e., the pronouncement of a legally binding judgment upon the parties to the dispute).

Federal court jurisdiction is limited to the types of cases listed in the Constitution and specifically provided by Congress. For the most part, federal courts only hear:

- cases in which the United States is a party[2];
- cases involving violations of the U.S. Constitution or federal laws (under federal-question jurisdiction[3]);
- cases between citizens of different states if the amount in controversy *exceeds* $75,000 (under diversity jurisdiction[4]); and
- bankruptcy, copyright, patent, and maritime law cases.

State courts, in contrast, have broad jurisdiction, so the cases individual citizens are likely to be involved in (e.g., robberies, traffic violations, contracts, and family disputes) are usually heard and decided in state courts. The only cases state courts are not allowed to hear are lawsuits against the United States and those involving certain specific federal laws: criminal, antitrust, bankruptcy, patent, copyright, and some maritime law cases.

In many cases, both federal and state courts have jurisdiction whereby the plaintiff (i.e., the party initiating the suit) can choose whether to file their claim in state or federal court.

Criminal cases involving federal laws can be tried only in federal court, but most criminal cases involve violations of state law and are tried in state court. Robbery is a crime, but what law makes it is a crime? Except for certain exceptions, state laws, not federal laws, make robbery a crime. There are only a few federal laws about robbery, such as the law that makes it a federal crime to rob a bank whose deposits are insured by a federal agency. Examples of other federal crimes are the transport of illegal drugs into the country or across state lines and using the U.S. mail system to defraud consumers.

Crimes committed on federal property (e.g., national parks or military reservations) are prosecuted in federal court.

Federal courts may hear cases concerning state laws if the issue is whether the state law violates the federal Constitution. Suppose a state law forbids slaughtering animals outside of certain limited areas. A neighborhood association brings a case in state court against a defendant who sacrifices chickens in their backyard. When the court issues an order (i.e., an injunction[5]) forbidding the defendant from further sacrifices, the defendant challenges the state law in federal court as an unconstitutional infringement of religious freedom.

Some conduct is illegal under both federal and state laws. For example, federal laws prohibit employment discrimination, and the states have added additional legal restrictions. A person can file their claim in either federal or state court under federal law or federal and state laws. A case that only involves a state law can be brought only in state court.

Appeals for review of actions by federal administrative agencies are federal civil cases.

For example, if the Environmental Protection Agency, over the objection of area residents, issued a permit to a paper mill to discharge water used in its milling process into the Scenic River, the residents may appeal and have the federal court of appeals review the agency's decision.

---

[1] *jurisdiction* – 1) the legal authority of a court to hear and decide specific types of case; 2) the geographic area over which the court has the authority to decide cases.

[2] *parties* – the plaintiff and the defendant in a lawsuit.

[3] *federal-question jurisdiction* – the federal district courts' authorization to hear and decide cases arising under the Constitution, laws, or treaties of the United States.

[4] *diversity jurisdiction* – the federal district courts' authority to hear and decide civil cases involving plaintiffs and defendants who are citizens of different states (or U.S. citizens and foreign nationals) and meet specific statutory requirements.

[5] *injunction* – a judge's order that a party takes or refrain from taking a particular action. An injunction may be preliminary until the outcome of a case is determined or permanent.

Appendix: U.S. Court Systems – Federal and State Courts

Organization of the federal courts

Congress has divided the country into 94 federal judicial districts, with each having a U.S. district court. The U.S. district courts are the federal trial courts -- where federal cases are tried, witnesses testify, and juries serve.

Each district has a U.S. bankruptcy court, which is part of the district court that administers the U.S. bankruptcy laws.

Congress uses state boundaries to help define the districts. Some districts cover an entire state, like Idaho. Other districts cover just part of a state, like the Northern District of California. Congress placed each of the ninety-four districts in one of twelve regional circuits whereby each circuit has a court of appeals. The losing party can petition the court of appeals to review the case to determine if the district judge applied the law correctly.

There is a U.S. Court of Appeals for the Federal Circuit, whose jurisdiction is defined by subject matter rather than geography. It hears appeals from certain courts and agencies, such as the U.S. Court of International Trade, the U.S. Court of Federal Claims, and the U.S. Patent and Trademark Office, and certain types of cases from the district courts (mainly lawsuits claiming that patents have been infringed).

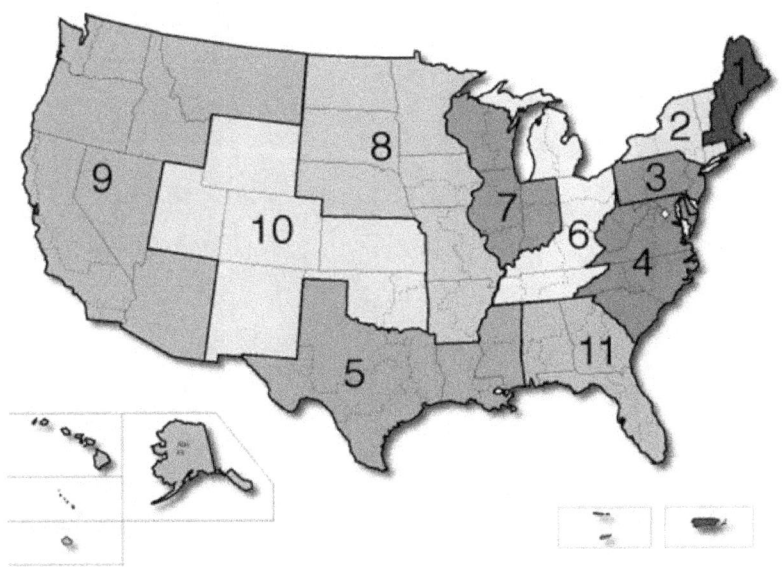

Twelve regional federal circuits

The Supreme Court in Washington, D.C., is the highest court in the nation. The losing party can petition in a case in the court of appeals (or, sometimes, in a state supreme court), can petition the Supreme Court to hear an appeal.

Unlike a court of appeals, the Supreme Court does not have to hear the case. The Supreme Court hears only a small percentage of the cases it is asked to review.

Notes for active learning

How Civil Cases Move Through the Federal Courts

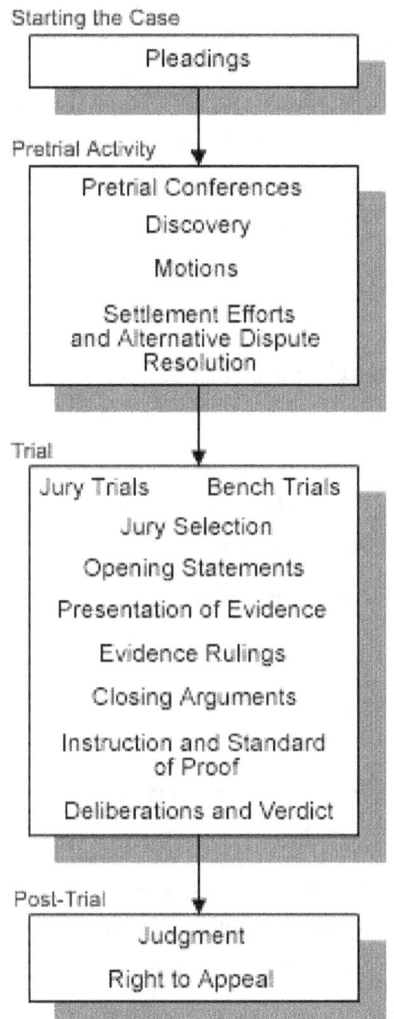

A federal civil case begins when a person, or their legal representative, files a paper with the clerk of the court that asserts another person's wrongful act injured the person. In legal terminology, the plaintiff files a *complaint* against the defendant.

The defendant files an *answer* to the complaint. These written statements of the party's positions are called pleadings. In some circumstances, the defendant may file a *motion* instead of an answer; the motion asks the court to take some action, such as dismiss the case or require the plaintiff to explain more clearly what the lawsuit is about.

Jury trials

In a jury trial, the jury decides what happened, and to apply the legal standards, the judge tells them to apply to reach a verdict. The plaintiff presents evidence supporting its view of the case, and the defendant presents evidence rebutting the plaintiff's evidence or supporting its view of the case. From these presentations, the jury must decide what happened and applied the law to those facts.

The jury never decides what law applies to the case; that is the role of the judge. For example, in a discrimination case where the plaintiff alleged that their workplace was hostile, the judge tells the jury the legal standard for a hostile environment.

The jury would have to decide whether the plaintiff's description of events was true and whether those events met the legal standard. A trial jury, or petit jury, may consist of six to twelve jurors in a civil case.

Bench trials

If the parties agree not to have a *jury trial* and leave the fact-finding to the judge, the trial is a *bench trial*. In bench and jury trials, the judge ensures the correct legal standards are followed.

In contrast to a jury trial, the judge decides the facts and renders the verdict in a *bench trial*.

For example, in a discrimination case in which the plaintiff alleged a hostile environment, the judge would determine the legal standard for a hostile environment and decide whether the plaintiff's description of events was true and whether those events met the legal standard.

Some kinds of cases always have bench trials. For example, there is never a jury trial if the plaintiff is seeking an injunction, an order from the judge that the defendant does, or stop doing something, as opposed to monetary damages.

Some statutes provide that a judge must decide the facts in certain types of cases.

Jury selection

A jury trial begins with the selection of jurors. Citizens are selected for jury service through a process set out in laws passed by Congress and in the federal rules of procedure.

First, citizens are called to court to be available to serve on juries. These citizens are selected at random from sources, in most districts, lists of registered voters, which may be augmented by other sources, such as lists of licensed drivers in the judicial district.

The judge and the lawyers choose who will serve on the jury.

To choose the jurors, the judge and sometimes the lawyers ask prospective jurors questions to determine if they will decide the case fairly, a process known as *voir dire*.

The lawyers may request that the judge excuse jurors they think may not be impartial, such as those who know a party in the case or who have had an experience that might make them favor one side over the other. These requests for rejecting jurors are *challenges for cause*.

The lawyers may request that the judge excuse a certain number of jurors without reason; these requests are *peremptory challenges*.

Instructions and standard of proof

Following the closing arguments, the judge gives instructions to the jury, explaining the relevant law, how the law applies to the case, and what questions the jury must decide.

How sure do jurors have to be before they reach a verdict? One important instruction the judge gives the jury is the standard of proof they must follow in deciding the case.

The courts, through their decisions, and Congress, through statutes, have established standards by which facts must be proven in criminal and civil cases.

In civil cases, to decide for the plaintiff, the jury must determine by a *preponderance of the evidence* that the defendant failed to perform a legal duty and violated the plaintiff's rights. A preponderance of the evidence means that, based on the evidence, the evidence favors the plaintiff more (even if only slightly) than it favors the defendant.

If the evidence in favor of the plaintiff could be placed on one side of a scale and that in favor of the defendant on the other, the plaintiff would win if the evidence in favor of the plaintiff was heavy enough to tip the scale. If the two sides were even, or if the scale tipped for the defendant, the defendant would win.

Judgment

In civil cases, if the jury (or judge) decides in favor of the plaintiff, the result usually is that the defendant must pay the plaintiff money or damages. The judge orders the defendant to pay the decided amount. Sometimes the defendant is ordered to take some specific action that will restore the plaintiff's rights. If the defendant wins the case, there is nothing more the trial court needs to do as the case is disposed of and the defendant is held not liable.

Right to appeal

The losing party in a federal civil case has a right to appeal the verdict to the U.S. court of appeals (i.e., Federal Circuit Courts) and ask the court to review the case to determine whether the trial was conducted properly. The losing party in the state trial court has a right to appeal the verdict to the state court of appeal.

The grounds for appeal usually are that the federal district (or state) judge made an error, either in the procedure (e.g., admitting improper evidence) or interpreting the law. The government may appeal in civil cases, as any other party may. Neither party may appeal if there was no trial -- parties settled their civil case out of court.

Notes for active learning

How Criminal Cases Move Through the Federal Courts

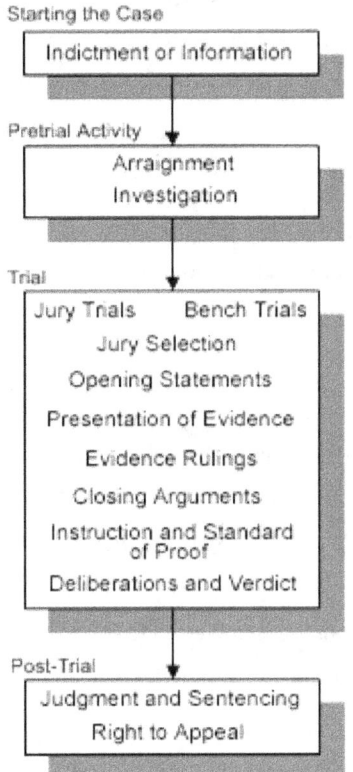

Indictment or information

A criminal case formally begins with an indictment or information, which is a formal accusation that a person committed a crime.

An indictment may be obtained when a lawyer (i.e., prosecutor) for the executive branch of the U.S. government (i.e., U.S. attorney or assistant U.S. attorney) present evidence to a federal grand jury that, according to the government, indicates a person committed a crime.

The U.S. attorney tries to convince the grand jury that there is enough evidence to show that the person probably committed the crime and should be formally accused. If the grand jury agrees, it issues an indictment.

A grand jury is different from a trial jury or petit jury.

A grand jury determines whether the person may be tried for a crime; a petit jury listens to the evidence presented at the trial and determines whether the defendant is guilty.

Petit is French for "small"; petit juries usually consist of twelve jurors in criminal cases.

Grand is French for "large"; grand juries have from sixteen to twenty-three jurors.

Grand jury indictments are most often used for *felonies* (i.e., punishable by imprisonment of more than a year or by death) such as bank robberies or sales of illegal drugs.

Grand jury indictments are not necessary to prosecute *misdemeanors* (i.e., less serious than a felony but more serious than an infraction) and are necessary for felonies.

For lesser crimes, the U.S. attorney issues an *information* that substitutes for an indictment. For example, speeding on a highway in a national park is a misdemeanor.

An information is used when a defendant waives an indictment by a grand jury.

Arraignment

After the grand jury issues the indictment, the accused (i.e., defendant) is summoned to court or arrested (if not already in custody). The next step is an arraignment, a proceeding in which the defendant is brought before a judge, told of the charges they are accused of, and asked to plead guilty or not guilty. If the defendant's plea is guilty, a time is set for the defendant to return to court to be sentenced.

If the defendant pleads "not guilty," the time is set for the trial.

A defendant may enter a plea bargain with the prosecution--usually by agreeing to plead guilty to some but not all charges or lesser charges. The prosecution drops the remaining charges.

About nine out of ten defendants in criminal cases plead guilty.

Investigation

In a criminal case, a defense lawyer conducts a thorough investigation before trial, interviewing witnesses, visiting the crime scene, and examining physical evidence. An important part of this investigation is determining whether the evidence the government plans to use to prove its case was obtained legally.

The Fourth Amendment to the Constitution forbids unreasonable searches and seizures. To enforce this protection, the Supreme Court has decided that illegally seized evidence cannot be used at trial for most purposes.

For example, if the police seize evidence from a defendant's home without a search warrant, the lawyer for the defendant can ask the court to exclude the evidence from use at trial. The court holds a hearing to determine whether the search was unreasonable.

If the court rules that key evidence was seized illegally and cannot be used, the government often drops the charges against the defendant.

If the government has a strong case and the court ruled that the evidence was obtained legally, the defendant may decide to plead guilty rather than go to trial, where a conviction is likely.

Deliberations and verdict

After receiving its instructions from the judge, the jury retires to the jury room to discuss the evidence and reach a verdict (a decision on the factual issues). A criminal jury verdict must be unanimous; all jurors must agree that the defendant is guilty or not guilty.

If the jurors cannot agree, the judge declares a mistrial, and the prosecutor must decide whether to ask the court to dismiss the case or have it presented to another jury.

Judgment and sentencing

In federal criminal cases, if the jury (or judge, if there is no jury) decides that the defendant is guilty, the judge sets a date for a sentencing hearing. In federal criminal cases, the jury does not decide whether the defendant will go to prison or for how long; the judge does.

In federal death penalty cases, the jury does decide whether the defendant will receive a death sentence. Sentencing statutes passed by Congress control the judge's sentencing decision. Additionally, judges use Sentencing Guidelines, issued by the U.S. Sentencing Commission, as a source of advice as to the proper sentence. The guidelines consider the nature of the offense and the offender's criminal history.

A presentence report, prepared by one of the court's probation officers, provides the judge with information about the offender and the offense, including the sentence recommended by the guidelines. After determining the sentence, the judge signs a judgment, including the plea, the verdict, and sentence.

Right to appeal

A defendant who is found guilty in a federal criminal trial has a right to appeal the decision to the U.S. court of appeals, that is, ask the court of appeals to review the case to determine whether the trial was conducted properly. The grounds for appeal are usually that the district judge is said to have made an error, either in a procedure (admitting improper evidence, for example) or interpreting the law.

A defendant who pled guilty may not appeal the conviction.

A defendant who pled guilty may have the right to appeal their sentence.

The government may not appeal if a defendant in a criminal case is found not guilty because the Double Jeopardy Clause of the Fifth Amendment to the Constitution provides that no person shall "be twice put in jeopardy of life or limb" for the same offense.

This reflects society's belief that, even if a subsequent trial might finally find a defendant guilty, it is not proper for the government to harass an acquitted defendant through repeated retrials.

However, the government may sometimes appeal a sentence.

Notes for active learning

How Civil and Criminal Appeals Move Through the Federal Courts

- Assignment of Judges
- Alternative Dispute Resolution (ADR)
- Review of Lower Court Decision
- Oral Argument
- Decision
- The Supreme Court of the United States

Assignment of judges

The courts of appeals usually assign cases to a panel of three judges. The panel decides the case for the entire court. Sometimes, when the parties request it or a question of unusual importance, the judges on the appeals court assemble *en banc* (a rare event).

Review of a lower court decision

In making its decision, the panel reviews key parts of the record. The record consists of the documents filed in the case at trial and the transcript of the trial proceedings. The panel learns about the lawyers' legal arguments from the lawyers' briefs.

Briefs are written documents that each side submits to explain its case and tell why the court should decide in its favor.

Oral argument

If the court permits oral argument, the lawyers for each side have a limited amount of time (typically between 15 to 30 minutes) to argue (i.e., advocate and explain) their case to the judges (or justices at the highest court in the jurisdiction) in a formal courtroom session. The judges (or justices for the highest court in the jurisdiction) frequently question the attorneys about the relevant law as it applies to the facts and issues in the case before them.

A court of appeals differs from the federal trial courts. There are no jurors, witnesses, or court reporters. The lawyers for each side, but not the parties, are usually present in the courtroom.

Decision

After the submission of briefs and oral arguments, the judges discuss the case privately, consider relevant *precedents* (court decisions from higher courts in prior cases with similar facts and legal issues), and reach a decision. Courts are required to follow precedents.

For example, a U.S. court of appeals must follow the U.S. Supreme Court's decisions; a district court must follow the decisions of the U.S. Supreme Court and the decisions of the court of appeals of its circuit.

Courts are influenced by decisions they are not required to follow, such as the decisions of other circuits. Courts follow precedent unless they set forth reasons for the diversion.

At least two of the three judges on the panel must agree on a decision. One judge who agrees with the decision is chosen to write an opinion, which announces and explains the decision.

If a judge on the panel disagrees with the majority's opinion, the judge may write a dissent, giving reasons for disagreeing.

Many appellate opinions are published in books of opinions, called reporters. The opinions are read carefully by other judges and lawyers looking for precedents to guide them in their cases.

The accumulated judicial opinions make up a body of law known as *case law*, which is usually an accurate predictor of how future cases will be decided.

For decisions that the judges believe are important to the parties and contribute little to the law, the appeals courts frequently use short, unsigned opinions that often are not published.

If the court of appeals decides that the trial judge incorrectly interpreted the law or followed incorrect procedures, it reverses the district court's decision.

For example, the court of appeals could hold that the district judge allowed the jury to base its decision on evidence that never should have been admitted, and thus the defendant cannot be guilty.

Most of the time, courts of appeals uphold, rather than the reverse, district court decisions.

Sometimes when a higher court reverses the decision of the district court, it sends the case back (i.e., *remand* the case) to the lower court for another trial.

For example, *Miranda v. Arizona* case (1966), the Supreme Court ruled 5-4 that Ernesto Miranda's confession could not be used as evidence because he had not been advised of his right to remain silent or of his right to have a lawyer present during questioning.

However, the government did have other evidence against him. The case was remanded for a new trial, in which the improperly obtained confession was not used as evidence, but the other evidence convicted Miranda.

The Supreme Court of the United States

The Supreme Court is the highest in the nation. It is a different kind of appeals court; its major function is not correcting errors made by trial judges but clarifying the law in cases of national importance or when lower courts disagree about interpreting the Constitution or federal laws.

The Supreme Court does not have to hear every case that it is asked to review. Each year, losing parties ask the Supreme Court to review about 8,000 cases.

Almost all cases come to the Court as a *petition for writ of certiorari*. The court selects only about 80 to 120 of the most significant cases to review with oral arguments.

Supreme Court decisions establish a precedent for interpreting the Constitution and federal laws; holdings that state and federal courts must follow.

The power of judicial review makes the Supreme Court's role in our government vital. Judicial review is the power of a court when deciding a case to declare that a law passed by a legislature or action by the executive branch is invalid because it is inconsistent with the Constitution.

Although district courts, courts of appeals, and state courts can exercise the power of judicial review, their decisions about federal law are always subject, on appeal, to review by the Supreme Court.

When the Supreme Court declares a law unconstitutional, its decision can only be overruled by a later decision of the Supreme Court or Amendment to the Constitution.

Seven of the twenty-seven Amendments to the Constitution have invalidated the decisions of the Supreme Court. However, most Supreme Court cases do not concern the constitutionality of laws, but the interpretation of laws passed by Congress.

Although Congress has steadily increased the number of district and appeals court judges over the years, the Supreme Court has remained the same size since 1869. It consists of a Chief Justice and eight associate justices.

Like the federal court of appeals and federal district judges, the Supreme Court justices are appointed by the President with the Senate's *advice and consent*.

Unlike the judges in the courts of appeals, Supreme Court justices never sit on panels. Absent recusal, nine justices hear cases, and a majority ruling decides cases.

The Supreme Court begins its annual session, or term, on the first Monday of October. The term lasts until the Court has announced its decisions in cases where it has heard an argument that term—usually late June or early July.

During the term, the Court, sitting for two weeks at a time, hears oral arguments on Monday through Wednesday and holds private conferences to discuss the cases, reach decisions, and begin preparing the written opinions that explain its decisions.

Most decisions and opinions are released in the late spring and early summer.

Standards of review for federal courts

Standard of review	De novo	Clearly erroneous	Abuse of discretion
Type of decision under review	Question of the law	Question of fact	Discretionary action
Lower-court decision maker	Trial judge	Trial judge	Trial judge
Deference given to lower court	No deference	Substantial deference	Extreme deference
Party typically benefitted	Appellant	Appellee	Appellee
Definition	An appellate court reviews the legal question anew and independently, without regard to the conclusions reached by the trial court. "When *de novo* review is compelled, no form of appellate deference is acceptable." *Salve Regina College v. Russell*, (1991).	A finding is 'clearly erroneous' when although there is evidence to support it, the reviewing court on the entire evidence is left with the definite and firm conviction that a mistake has been committed. *United States v. United States Gypsum Co.*, (1948) "If the district court's account of the evidence is plausible in light of the record viewed in its entirety, the court of appeals may not reverse it even though convinced that had it been sitting as the trier of fact, it would have weighed the evidence differently. When there are two permissible views of the evidence, the factfinder's choice between them cannot be clearly erroneous." *Anderson v. Bessemer City*, (1985).	Generally, an abuse of discretion only occurs where no reasonable person could take the view adopted by the trial court. If reasonable persons could differ, no abuse of discretion can be found. *Harrington v. DeVito*, (7th Cir. 1981) Under the abuse of discretion standard, a trial court's decision will not be disturbed unless the appellate court has a definite and firm conviction that the lower court made a clear error of judgment or exceeded the bounds of permissible choice in the circumstances. We will not alter a trial court's decision unless it can be shown that the court's decision was an arbitrary, capricious, whimsical, or manifestly unreasonable judgment. *Wright v. Abbott Laboratories, Inc.*, (10th Cir. 2001)
Examples	Motions for summary judgment, constitutional questions, statutory interpretation	Questions regarding who did what, where, and when; questions of intent and motive; questions of ultimate fact (such as negligence)	Rule 11 sanctions, attorney's fees, courtroom management, motions to compel, injunctions, and temporary restraining orders.

Appendix: The Constitution of the United States (a transcription)

The Constitution of the United States (*a transcription*)

THE U.S. NATIONAL ARCHIVES & RECORDS ADMINISTRATION
www.archives.gov

The following text is a transcription of the Constitution as it was inscribed by Jacob Shallus on parchment (the document on display in the Rotunda at the National Archives Museum.) The spelling and punctuation reflect the original.

The Constitution of the United States: A Transcription

The following text is a transcription of the Constitution as it was inscribed by Jacob Shallus on parchment (displayed in the Rotunda at the National Archives Museum.) The authenticated text of the Constitution can be found on the website of the Government Printing Office.

We the People of the United States, in Order to form a more perfect Union, establish Justice, insure domestic Tranquility, provide for the common defence, promote the general Welfare, and secure the Blessings of Liberty to ourselves and our Posterity, do ordain and establish this Constitution for the United States of America.

Article. I

Section. 1.

All legislative Powers herein granted shall be vested in a Congress of the United States, which shall consist of a Senate and House of Representatives.

Section. 2.

The House of Representatives shall be composed of Members chosen every second Year by the People of the several States, and the Electors in each State shall have the Qualifications requisite for Electors of the most numerous Branch of the State Legislature.

No Person shall be a Representative who shall not have attained to the Age of twenty five Years, and been seven Years a Citizen of the United States, and who shall not, when elected, be an Inhabitant of that State in which he shall be chosen.

Representatives and direct Taxes shall be apportioned among the several States which may be included within this Union, according to their respective Numbers, which shall be determined by adding to the whole Number of free Persons, including those bound to Service for a Term of Years, and excluding Indians not taxed, three fifths of all other Persons. The actual Enumeration shall be made within three Years after the first Meeting of the Congress of the United States, and within every subsequent Term of ten Years, in such Manner as they shall by Law direct. The Number of Representatives shall not exceed one for every thirty Thousand, but each State shall have at Least one Representative; and until such enumeration shall be made, the State of New Hampshire shall be entitled to chuse three, Massachusetts eight, Rhode-Island and Providence

Plantations one, Connecticut five, New-York six, New Jersey four, Pennsylvania eight, Delaware one, Maryland six, Virginia ten, North Carolina five, South Carolina five, and Georgia three.

When vacancies happen in the Representation from any State, the Executive Authority thereof shall issue Writs of Election to fill such Vacancies.

The House of Representatives shall chuse their Speaker and other Officers; and shall have the sole Power of Impeachment.

Section. 3.

The Senate of the United States shall be composed of two Senators from each State, chosen by the Legislature thereof, for six Years; and each Senator shall have one Vote.

Immediately after they shall be assembled in Consequence of the first Election, they shall be divided as equally as may be into three Classes. The Seats of the Senators of the first Class shall be vacated at the Expiration of the second Year, of the second Class at the Expiration of the fourth Year, and of the third Class at the Expiration of the sixth Year, so that one third may be chosen every second Year; and if Vacancies happen by Resignation, or otherwise, during the Recess of the Legislature of any State, the Executive thereof may make temporary Appointments until the next Meeting of the Legislature, which shall then fill such Vacancies.

No Person shall be a Senator who shall not have attained to the Age of thirty Years, and been nine Years a Citizen of the United States, and who shall not, when elected, be an Inhabitant of that State for which he shall be chosen.

The Vice President of the United States shall be President of the Senate, but shall have no Vote, unless they be equally divided.

The Senate shall chuse their other Officers, and also a President pro tempore, in the Absence of the Vice President, or when he shall exercise the Office of President of the United States.

The Senate shall have the sole Power to try all Impeachments. When sitting for that Purpose, they shall be on Oath or Affirmation. When the President of the United States is tried, the Chief Justice shall preside: And no Person shall be convicted without the Concurrence of two thirds of the Members present.

Judgment in Cases of Impeachment shall not extend further than to removal from Office, and disqualification to hold and enjoy any Office of honor, Trust or Profit under the United States: but the Party convicted shall nevertheless be liable and subject to Indictment, Trial, Judgment and Punishment, according to Law.

Section. 4.

The Times, Places and Manner of holding Elections for Senators and Representatives, shall be prescribed in each State by the Legislature thereof; but the Congress may at any time by Law make or alter such Regulations, except as to the Places of chusing Senators.

The Congress shall assemble at least once in every Year, and such Meeting shall be on the first Monday in December, unless they shall by Law appoint a different Day.

Section. 5.

Each House shall be the Judge of the Elections, Returns and Qualifications of its own Members, and a Majority of each shall constitute a Quorum to do Business; but a smaller Number may adjourn from day to day, and may be authorized to compel the Attendance of absent Members, in such Manner, and under such Penalties as each House may provide.

Each House may determine the Rules of its Proceedings, punish its Members for disorderly Behaviour, and, with the Concurrence of two thirds, expel a Member.

Each House shall keep a Journal of its Proceedings, and from time to time publish the same, excepting such Parts as may in their Judgment require Secrecy; and the Yeas and Nays of the Members of either House on any question shall, at the Desire of one fifth of those Present, be entered on the Journal.

Neither House, during the Session of Congress, shall, without the Consent of the other, adjourn for more than three days, nor to any other Place than that in which the two Houses shall be sitting.

Section. 6.

The Senators and Representatives shall receive a Compensation for their Services, to be ascertained by Law, and paid out of the Treasury of the United States. They shall in all Cases, except Treason, Felony and Breach of the Peace, be privileged from Arrest during their Attendance at the Session of their respective Houses, and in going to and returning from the same; and for any Speech or Debate in either House, they shall not be questioned in any other Place.

No Senator or Representative shall, during the Time for which he was elected, be appointed to any civil Office under the Authority of the United States, which shall have been created, or the Emoluments whereof shall have been encreased during such time; and no Person holding any Office under the United States, shall be a Member of either House during his Continuance in Office.

Section. 7.

All Bills for raising Revenue shall originate in the House of Representatives; but the Senate may propose or concur with Amendments as on other Bills.

Every Bill which shall have passed the House of Representatives and the Senate, shall, before it become a Law, be presented to the President of the United States; If he approves he shall sign it, but if not he shall return it, with his Objections to that House in which it shall have originated, who shall enter the Objections at large on their Journal, and proceed to reconsider it. If after such Reconsideration two thirds of that House shall agree to pass the Bill, it shall be sent, together with the Objections, to the other House, by which it shall likewise be reconsidered, and if approved by two thirds of that House, it shall become a Law. But in all such Cases the Votes of both Houses shall be determined by yeas and Nays, and the Names of the Persons voting for and against the Bill shall be entered on the Journal of each House respectively. If any Bill shall not be returned by the President within ten Days (Sundays excepted) after it shall have been presented to him, the Same shall be a Law, in like Manner as if he had signed it, unless the Congress by their Adjournment prevent its Return, in which Case it shall not be a Law.

Every Order, Resolution, or Vote to which the Concurrence of the Senate and House of Representatives may be necessary (except on a question of Adjournment) shall be presented to the President of the United States; and before the Same shall take Effect, shall be approved by him, or being disapproved by him, shall be repassed by two thirds of the Senate and House of Representatives, according to the Rules and Limitations prescribed in the Case of a Bill.

Section. 8.

The Congress shall have Power To lay and collect Taxes, Duties, Imposts and Excises, to pay the Debts and provide for the common Defence and general Welfare of the United States; but all Duties, Imposts and Excises shall be uniform throughout the United States;

To borrow Money on the credit of the United States;

To regulate Commerce with foreign Nations, and among the several States, and with the Indian Tribes;

To establish an uniform Rule of Naturalization, and uniform Laws on the subject of Bankruptcies throughout the United States;

To coin Money, regulate the Value thereof, and of foreign Coin, and fix the Standard of Weights and Measures;

To provide for the Punishment of counterfeiting the Securities and current Coin of the United States;

To establish Post Offices and post Roads;

To promote the Progress of Science and useful Arts, by securing for limited Times to Authors and Inventors the exclusive Right to their respective Writings and Discoveries;

To constitute Tribunals inferior to the Supreme Court;

To define and punish Piracies and Felonies committed on the high Seas, and Offences against the Law of Nations;

To declare War, grant Letters of Marque and Reprisal, and make Rules concerning Captures on Land and Water;

To raise and support Armies, but no Appropriation of Money to that Use shall be for a longer Term than two Years;

To provide and maintain a Navy;

To make Rules for the Government and Regulation of the land and naval Forces;

To provide for calling forth the Militia to execute the Laws of the Union, suppress Insurrections and repel Invasions;

To provide for organizing, arming, and disciplining, the Militia, and for governing such Part of them as may be employed in the Service of the United States, reserving to the States respectively, the Appointment of the Officers, and the Authority of training the Militia according to the discipline prescribed by Congress;

To exercise exclusive Legislation in all Cases whatsoever, over such District (not exceeding ten Miles square) as may, by Cession of particular States, and the Acceptance of Congress, become the Seat of the Government of the United States, and to exercise like Authority over all Places purchased by the Consent of the Legislature of the State in which the Same shall be, for the Erection of Forts, Magazines, Arsenals, dock-Yards, and other needful Buildings;—And

To make all Laws which shall be necessary and proper for carrying into Execution the foregoing Powers, and all other Powers vested by this Constitution in the Government of the United States, or in any Department or Officer thereof.

Section. 9.

The Migration or Importation of such Persons as any of the States now existing shall think proper to admit, shall not be prohibited by the Congress prior to the Year one thousand eight hundred and eight, but a Tax or duty may be imposed on such Importation, not exceeding ten dollars for each Person.

The Privilege of the Writ of Habeas Corpus shall not be suspended, unless when in Cases of Rebellion or Invasion the public Safety may require it.

No Bill of Attainder or ex post facto Law shall be passed.

No Capitation, or other direct, Tax shall be laid, unless in Proportion to the Census or enumeration herein before directed to be taken.

No Tax or Duty shall be laid on Articles exported from any State.

No Preference shall be given by any Regulation of Commerce or Revenue to the Ports of one State over those of another: nor shall Vessels bound to, or from, one State, be obliged to enter, clear, or pay Duties in another.

No Money shall be drawn from the Treasury, but in Consequence of Appropriations made by Law; and a regular Statement and Account of the Receipts and Expenditures of all public Money shall be published from time to time.

No Title of Nobility shall be granted by the United States: And no Person holding any Office of Profit or Trust under them, shall, without the Consent of the Congress, accept of any present, Emolument, Office, or Title, of any kind whatever, from any King, Prince, or foreign State.

Section. 10.

No State shall enter into any Treaty, Alliance, or Confederation; grant Letters of Marque and Reprisal; coin Money; emit Bills of Credit; make any Thing but gold and silver Coin a Tender in Payment of Debts; pass any Bill of Attainder, ex post facto Law, or Law impairing the Obligation of Contracts, or grant any Title of Nobility.

No State shall, without the Consent of the Congress, lay any Imposts or Duties on Imports or Exports, except what may be absolutely necessary for executing it's inspection Laws: and the net

Produce of all Duties and Imposts, laid by any State on Imports or Exports, shall be for the Use of the Treasury of the United States; and all such Laws shall be subject to the Revision and Controul of the Congress.

No State shall, without the Consent of Congress, lay any Duty of Tonnage, keep Troops, or Ships of War in time of Peace, enter into any Agreement or Compact with another State, or with a foreign Power, or engage in War, unless actually invaded, or in such imminent Danger as will not admit of delay.

Article. II

Section. 1.

The executive Power shall be vested in a President of the United States of America. He shall hold his Office during the Term of four Years, and, together with the Vice President, chosen for the same Term, be elected, as follows

Each State shall appoint, in such Manner as the Legislature thereof may direct, a Number of Electors, equal to the whole Number of Senators and Representatives to which the State may be entitled in the Congress: but no Senator or Representative, or Person holding an Office of Trust or Profit under the United States, shall be appointed an Elector.

The Electors shall meet in their respective States, and vote by Ballot for two Persons, of whom one at least shall not be an Inhabitant of the same State with themselves. And they shall make a List of all the Persons voted for, and of the Number of Votes for each; which List they shall sign and certify, and transmit sealed to the Seat of the Government of the United States, directed to the President of the Senate. The President of the Senate shall, in the Presence of the Senate and House of Representatives, open all the Certificates, and the Votes shall then be counted. The Person having the greatest Number of Votes shall be the President, if such Number be a Majority of the whole Number of Electors appointed; and if there be more than one who have such Majority, and have an equal Number of Votes, then the House of Representatives shall immediately chuse by Ballot one of them for President; and if no Person have a Majority, then from the five highest on the List the said House shall in like Manner chuse the President. But in chusing the President, the Votes shall be taken by States, the Representation from each State having one Vote; A quorum for this Purpose shall consist of a Member or Members from two thirds of the States, and a Majority of all the States shall be necessary to a Choice. In every Case, after the Choice of the President, the Person having the greatest Number of Votes of the Electors shall be the Vice President. But if there should remain two or more who have equal Votes, the Senate shall chuse from them by Ballot the Vice President.

The Congress may determine the Time of chusing the Electors, and the Day on which they shall give their Votes; which Day shall be the same throughout the United States.

No Person except a natural born Citizen, or a Citizen of the United States, at the time of the Adoption of this Constitution, shall be eligible to the Office of President; neither shall any Person be eligible to that Office who shall not have attained to the Age of thirty five Years, and been fourteen Years a Resident within the United States.

In Case of the Removal of the President from Office, or of his Death, Resignation, or Inability to discharge the Powers and Duties of the said Office, the Same shall devolve on the Vice President, and the Congress may by Law provide for the Case of Removal, Death, Resignation or Inability, both of the President and Vice President, declaring what Officer shall then act as President, and such Officer shall act accordingly, until the Disability be removed, or a President shall be elected.

The President shall, at stated Times, receive for his Services, a Compensation, which shall neither be encreased nor diminished during the Period for which he shall have been elected, and he shall not receive within that Period any other Emolument from the United States, or any of them.

Before he enters on the Execution of his Office, he shall take the following Oath or Affirmation:—"I do solemnly swear (or affirm) that I will faithfully execute the Office of President of the United States, and will to the best of my Ability, preserve, protect and defend the Constitution of the United States."

Section. 2.

The President shall be Commander in Chief of the Army and Navy of the United States, and of the Militia of the several States, when called into the actual Service of the United States; he may require the Opinion, in writing, of the principal Officer in each of the executive Departments, upon any Subject relating to the Duties of their respective Offices, and he shall have Power to grant Reprieves and Pardons for Offences against the United States, except in Cases of Impeachment.

He shall have Power, by and with the Advice and Consent of the Senate, to make Treaties, provided two thirds of the Senators present concur; and he shall nominate, and by and with the Advice and Consent of the Senate, shall appoint Ambassadors, other public Ministers and Consuls, Judges of the supreme Court, and all other Officers of the United States, whose Appointments are not herein otherwise provided for, and which shall be established by Law: but the Congress may by Law vest the Appointment of such inferior Officers, as they think proper, in the President alone, in the Courts of Law, or in the Heads of Departments.

The President shall have Power to fill up all Vacancies that may happen during the Recess of the Senate, by granting Commissions which shall expire at the End of their next Session.

Section. 3.

He shall from time to time give to the Congress Information of the State of the Union, and recommend to their Consideration such Measures as he shall judge necessary and expedient; he may, on extraordinary Occasions, convene both Houses, or either of them, and in Case of Disagreement between them, with Respect to the Time of Adjournment, he may adjourn them to such Time as he shall think proper; he shall receive Ambassadors and other public Ministers; he shall take Care that the Laws be faithfully executed, and shall Commission all the Officers of the United States.

Section. 4.

The President, Vice President and all civil Officers of the United States, shall be removed from Office on Impeachment for, and Conviction of, Treason, Bribery, or other high Crimes and Misdemeanors.

Article III

Section. 1.

The judicial Power of the United States, shall be vested in one supreme Court, and in such inferior Courts as the Congress may from time to time ordain and establish. The Judges, both of the supreme and inferior Courts, shall hold their Offices during good Behaviour, and shall, at stated Times, receive for their Services, a Compensation, which shall not be diminished during their Continuance in Office.

Section. 2.

The judicial Power shall extend to all Cases, in Law and Equity, arising under this Constitution, the Laws of the United States, and Treaties made, or which shall be made, under their Authority;—to all Cases affecting Ambassadors, other public Ministers and Consuls;—to all Cases of admiralty and maritime Jurisdiction;—to Controversies to which the United States shall be a Party;—to Controversies between two or more States;—between a State and Citizens of another State,—between Citizens of different States,—between Citizens of the same State claiming Lands under Grants of different States, and between a State, or the Citizens thereof, and foreign States, Citizens or Subjects.

In all Cases affecting Ambassadors, other public Ministers and Consuls, and those in which a State shall be Party, the supreme Court shall have original Jurisdiction. In all the other Cases before mentioned, the supreme Court shall have appellate Jurisdiction, both as to Law and Fact, with such Exceptions, and under such Regulations as the Congress shall make.

The Trial of all Crimes, except in Cases of Impeachment, shall be by Jury; and such Trial shall be held in the State where the said Crimes shall have been committed; but when not committed within any State, the Trial shall be at such Place or Places as the Congress may by Law have directed.

Section. 3.

Treason against the United States, shall consist only in levying War against them, or in adhering to their Enemies, giving them Aid and Comfort. No Person shall be convicted of Treason unless on the Testimony of two Witnesses to the same overt Act, or on Confession in open Court.

The Congress shall have Power to declare the Punishment of Treason, but no Attainder of Treason shall work Corruption of Blood, or Forfeiture except during the Life of the Person attainted.

Article. IV

Section. 1.

Full Faith and Credit shall be given in each State to the public Acts, Records, and judicial Proceedings of every other State. And the Congress may by general Laws prescribe the Manner in which such Acts, Records and Proceedings shall be proved, and the Effect thereof.

Section. 2.

The Citizens of each State shall be entitled to all Privileges and Immunities of Citizens in the several States.

A Person charged in any State with Treason, Felony, or other Crime, who shall flee from Justice, and be found in another State, shall on Demand of the executive Authority of the State from which he fled, be delivered up, to be removed to the State having Jurisdiction of the Crime.

No Person held to Service or Labour in one State, under the Laws thereof, escaping into another, shall, in Consequence of any Law or Regulation therein, be discharged from such Service or Labour, but shall be delivered up on Claim of the Party to whom such Service or Labour may be due.

Section. 3.

New States may be admitted by the Congress into this Union; but no new State shall be formed or erected within the Jurisdiction of any other State; nor any State be formed by the Junction of two or more States, or Parts of States, without the Consent of the Legislatures of the States concerned as well as of the Congress.

The Congress shall have Power to dispose of and make all needful Rules and Regulations respecting the Territory or other Property belonging to the United States; and nothing in this Constitution shall be so construed as to Prejudice any Claims of the United States, or of any particular State.

Section. 4.

The United States shall guarantee to every State in this Union a Republican Form of Government, and shall protect each of them against Invasion; and on Application of the Legislature, or of the Executive (when the Legislature cannot be convened), against domestic Violence.

Article. V

The Congress, whenever two thirds of both Houses shall deem it necessary, shall propose Amendments to this Constitution, or, on the Application of the Legislatures of two thirds of the several States, shall call a Convention for proposing Amendments, which, in either Case, shall be valid to all Intents and Purposes, as Part of this Constitution, when ratified by the Legislatures of three fourths of the several States, or by Conventions in three fourths thereof, as the one or the other Mode of Ratification may be proposed by the Congress; Provided that no Amendment which may be made prior to the Year One thousand eight hundred and eight shall in any Manner affect the first and fourth Clauses in the Ninth Section of the first Article; and that no State, without its Consent, shall be deprived of its equal Suffrage in the Senate.

Article. VI

All Debts contracted and Engagements entered into, before the Adoption of this Constitution, shall be as valid against the United States under this Constitution, as under the Confederation.

This Constitution, and the Laws of the United States which shall be made in Pursuance thereof; and all Treaties made, or which shall be made, under the Authority of the United States, shall be the supreme Law of the Land; and the Judges in every State shall be bound thereby, any Thing in the Constitution or Laws of any State to the Contrary notwithstanding.

The Senators and Representatives before mentioned, and the Members of the several State Legislatures, and all executive and judicial Officers, both of the United States and of the several States, shall be bound by Oath or Affirmation, to support this Constitution; but no religious Test shall ever be required as a Qualification to any Office or public Trust under the United States.

Article. VII

The Ratification of the Conventions of nine States, shall be sufficient for the Establishment of this Constitution between the States so ratifying the Same.

The Word, "the," being interlined between the seventh and eighth Lines of the first Page, The Word "Thirty" being partly written on an Erazure in the fifteenth Line of the first Page, The Words "is tried" being interlined between the thirty second and thirty third Lines of the first Page and the Word "the" being interlined between the forty third and forty fourth Lines of the second Page.

Attest William Jackson Secretary, done in Convention by the Unanimous Consent of the States present the Seventeenth Day of September in the Year of our Lord one thousand seven hundred and Eighty seven and of the Independance of the United States of America the Twelfth In witness whereof We have hereunto subscribed our Names, G°. Washington, *Presidt and deputy from Virginia*

Delaware
Geo: Read
Gunning Bedford jun
John Dickinson
Richard Bassett
Jaco: Broom

Maryland
James McHenry
Dan of St Thos. Jenifer
Danl. Carroll

Virginia
John Blair
James Madison Jr.

North Carolina
Wm. Blount
Richd. Dobbs Spaight
Hu Williamson

South Carolina
J. Rutledge
Charles Cotesworth Pinckney
Charles Pinckney
Pierce Butler

Georgia
William Few
Abr Baldwin

New Hampshire
John Langdon
Nicholas Gilman

Massachusetts
Nathaniel Gorham
Rufus King

Connecticut
Wm. Saml. Johnson
Roger Sherman

New York
Alexander Hamilton

New Jersey
Wil: Livingston
David Brearley
Wm. Paterson
Jona: Dayton

Pensylvania
B Franklin
Thomas Mifflin
Robt. Morris
Geo. Clymer
Thos. FitzSimons
Jared Ingersoll
James Wilson
Gouv Morris

Enactment of the Bill of Rights of the United States of America (1791)

The first ten Amendments to the Constitution make up the Bill of Rights. Written by James Madison in response to calls from several states for greater constitutional protection for individual liberties, the Bill of Rights lists specific prohibitions on governmental power. The Virginia Declaration of Rights, written by George Mason, strongly influenced Madison.

One of the contention points between Federalists and Anti-Federalists was the Constitution's lack of a bill of rights that would place specific limits on government power.

Federalists argued that the Constitution did not need a bill of rights because the people and the states kept powers not explicitly given to the federal government.

Anti-Federalists held that a *bill of rights* was necessary to safeguard individual liberty.

Madison, then a member of the U.S. House of Representatives, went through the Constitution itself, making changes where he thought most appropriate.

Several Representatives, led by Roger Sherman, objected that Congress had no authority to change the wording of the Constitution. Therefore, Madison's changes were presented as a list of amendments that would follow Article VII.

The House approved 17 amendments. Of these 17, the Senate approved 12. Those 12 were sent to the states for approval in August of 1789. Of those 12 proposed amendments, 10 were quickly ratified. Virginia's legislature became the last to ratify the Amendments on December 15, 1791. These Amendments are the Bill of Rights.

The Bill of Rights is a list of limits on government power. For example, what the Founders saw as the natural right of individuals to speak and worship freely was protected by the First Amendment's prohibitions on Congress from making laws establishing a religion or abridging freedom of speech.

Another example is the natural right to be free from the government's unreasonable intrusion in one's home was safeguarded by the Fourth Amendment's warrant requirements.

Other precursors to the Bill of Rights include English documents such as the Magna Carta[1], the Petition of Rights, the English Bill of Rights, and the Massachusetts Body of Liberties.

The Magna Carta illustrates Compact Theory[1] as well as initial strides toward limited government. Its provisions address individual rights and political rights. Latin for "Great Charter," the Magna Carta was written by Barons in Runnymede, England, and forced on the King.

Although the protections were generally limited to the prerogatives of the Barons, the Magna Carta embodied the general principle that the King accepted limitations on his rule. These included the fundamental acknowledgment that the king was not above the law.

Included in the Magna Carta are protections for the English church, petitioning the king, freedom from the forced quarter of troops and unreasonable searches, due process and fair trial protections, and freedom from excessive fines. These protections can be found in the First, Third, Fourth, Fifth, Sixth, and Eighth Amendments to the Constitution.

The Magna Carta is the oldest compact in England. The Mayflower Compact, the Fundamental Orders of Connecticut, and the Albany Plan are examples from the American colonies.

The Articles of Confederation was a compact among the states, and the Constitution creates a compact based on a federal system between the national government, state governments, and the people. The Hayne-Webster Debate focused on the compact created by the Constitution.

---

[1] Philosophers including Thomas Hobbes, John Locke, and Jean-Jacques Rousseau theorized that peoples' condition in a "state of nature" (that is, outside of society) is one of freedom, but that freedom inevitably degrades into war, chaos, or debilitating competition without the benefit of a system of laws and government. They reasoned, therefore, that for their happiness, individuals willingly trade some of their natural freedom in exchange for the protections provided by the government.

The Bill of Rights: Amendments I–X

Amendment I

Congress shall make no law respecting an establishment of religion, or prohibiting the free exercise thereof; or abridging the freedom of speech, or of the press; or the right of the people peaceably to assemble, and to petition the government for a redress of grievances.

Amendment II

A well regulated militia, being necessary to the security of a free state, the right of the people to keep and bear arms, shall not be infringed.

Amendment III

No soldier shall, in time of peace be quartered in any house, without the consent of the owner, nor in time of war, but in a manner to be prescribed by law.

Amendment IV

The right of the people to be secure in their persons, houses, papers, and effects, against unreasonable searches and seizures, shall not be violated, and no warrants shall issue, but upon probable cause, supported by oath or affirmation, and particularly describing the place to be searched, and the persons or things to be seized.

Amendment V

No person shall be held to answer for a capital, or otherwise infamous crime, unless on a presentment or indictment of a grand jury, except in cases arising in the land or naval forces, or in the militia, when in actual service in time of war or public danger; nor shall any person be subject for the same offense to be twice put in jeopardy of life or limb; nor shall be compelled in any criminal case to be a witness against himself, nor be deprived of life, liberty, or property, without due process of law; nor shall private property be taken for public use, without just compensation.

Amendment VI

In all criminal prosecutions, the accused shall enjoy the right to a speedy and public trial, by an impartial jury of the state and district wherein the crime shall have been committed, which district shall have been previously ascertained by law, and to be informed of the nature and cause of the accusation; to be confronted with the witnesses against him; to have compulsory process for obtaining witnesses in his favor, and to have the assistance of counsel for his defense.

Amendment VII

In suits at common law, where the value in controversy shall exceed twenty dollars, the right of trial by jury shall be preserved, and no fact tried by a jury, shall be otherwise reexamined in any court of the United States, than according to the rules of the common law.

Amendment VIII

Excessive bail shall not be required, nor excessive fines imposed, nor cruel and unusual punishments inflicted.

Amendment IX

The enumeration in the Constitution, of certain rights, shall not be construed to deny or disparage others retained by the people.

Amendment X

The powers not delegated to the United States by the Constitution, nor prohibited by it to the states, are reserved to the states respectively, or to the people.

Constitutional Amendments XI–XXVII

AMENDMENT XI

Passed by Congress March 4, 1794. Ratified February 7, 1795.

Note: Article III, section 2, of the Constitution was modified by amendment 11.

The Judicial power of the United States shall not be construed to extend to any suit in law or equity, commenced or prosecuted against one of the United States by Citizens of another State, or by Citizens or Subjects of any Foreign State.

AMENDMENT XII

Passed by Congress December 9, 1803. Ratified June 15, 1804.

Note: A portion of Article II, section 1 of the Constitution was superseded by the 12th amendment.

The Electors shall meet in their respective states and vote by ballot for President and Vice-President, one of whom, at least, shall not be an inhabitant of the same state with themselves; they shall name in their ballots the person voted for as President, and in distinct ballots the person voted for as Vice-President, and they shall make distinct lists of all persons voted for as President, and of all persons voted for as Vice-President, and of the number of votes for each, which lists they shall sign and certify, and transmit sealed to the seat of the government of the United States, directed to the President of the Senate; -- the President of the Senate shall, in the presence of the Senate and House of Representatives, open all the certificates and the votes shall then be counted; -- The person having the greatest number of votes for President, shall be the President, if such number be a majority of the whole number of Electors appointed; and if no person have such majority, then from the persons having the highest numbers not exceeding three on the list of those voted for as President, the House of Representatives shall choose immediately, by ballot, the President. But in choosing the President, the votes shall be taken by states, the representation from each state having one vote; a quorum for this purpose shall consist of a member or members from two-thirds of the states, and a majority of all the states shall be necessary to a choice. [And if the House of Representatives shall not choose a President whenever the right of choice shall devolve upon them, before the fourth day of March next following, then the Vice-President shall act as President, as in case of the death or other constitutional disability of the President. --]* The person having the greatest number of votes as Vice-President, shall be the Vice-President, if such number be a majority of the whole number of Electors appointed, and if no person have a majority, then from the two highest numbers on the list, the Senate shall choose the Vice-President; a quorum for the purpose shall consist of two-thirds of the whole number of Senators, and a majority of the whole number shall be necessary to a choice. But no person constitutionally ineligible to the office of President shall be eligible to that of Vice-President of the United States.

*Superseded by section 3 of the 20th Amendment.

AMENDMENT XIII

Passed by Congress January 31, 1865. Ratified December 6, 1865.

Note: A portion of Article IV, section 2, of the Constitution was superseded by the 13th amendment.

Section 1.
Neither slavery nor involuntary servitude, except as a punishment for crime whereof the party shall have been duly convicted, shall exist within the United States, or any place subject to their jurisdiction.

Section 2.
Congress shall have power to enforce this article by appropriate legislation.

AMENDMENT XIV

Passed by Congress June 13, 1866. Ratified July 9, 1868.

Note: Article I, section 2, of the Constitution was modified by section 2 of the 14th amendment.

Section 1.
All persons born or naturalized in the United States, and subject to the jurisdiction thereof, are citizens of the United States and of the State wherein they reside. No State shall make or enforce any law which shall abridge the privileges or immunities of citizens of the United States; nor shall any State deprive any person of life, liberty, or property, without due process of law; nor deny to any person within its jurisdiction the equal protection of the laws.

Section 2.
Representatives shall be apportioned among the several States according to their respective numbers, counting the whole number of persons in each State, excluding Indians not taxed. But when the right to vote at any election for the choice of electors for President and Vice-President of the United States, Representatives in Congress, the Executive and Judicial officers of a State, or the members of the Legislature thereof, is denied to any of the male inhabitants of such State, being twenty-one years of age,* and citizens of the United States, or in any way abridged, except for participation in rebellion, or other crime, the basis of representation therein shall be reduced in the proportion which the number of such male citizens shall bear to the whole number of male citizens twenty-one years of age in such State.

Section 3.
No person shall be a Senator or Representative in Congress, or elector of President and Vice-President, or hold any office, civil or military, under the United States, or under any State, who, having previously taken an oath, as a member of Congress, or as an officer of the United States, or as a member of any State legislature, or as an executive or judicial officer of any State, to support the Constitution of the United States, shall have engaged in insurrection or rebellion against the same, or given aid or comfort to the enemies thereof. But Congress may by a vote of two-thirds of each House, remove such disability.

Section 4.

The validity of the public debt of the United States, authorized by law, including debts incurred for payment of pensions and bounties for services in suppressing insurrection or rebellion, shall not be questioned. But neither the United States nor any State shall assume or pay any debt or obligation incurred in aid of insurrection or rebellion against the United States, or any claim for the loss or emancipation of any slave; but all such debts, obligations and claims shall be held illegal and void.

Section 5.

The Congress shall have the power to enforce, by appropriate legislation, the provisions of this article.

*Changed by section 1 of the 26th Amendment.

AMENDMENT XV

Passed by Congress February 26, 1869. Ratified February 3, 1870.

Section 1.

The right of citizens of the United States to vote shall not be denied or abridged by the United States or by any State on account of race, color, or previous condition of servitude.

Section 2.

The Congress shall have the power to enforce this article by appropriate legislation.

AMENDMENT XVI

Passed by Congress July 2, 1909. Ratified February 3, 1913.

Note: Article I, section 9, of the Constitution was modified by amendment 16.

The Congress shall have power to lay and collect taxes on incomes, from whatever source derived, without apportionment among the several States, and without regard to any census or enumeration.

AMENDMENT XVII

Passed by Congress May 13, 1912. Ratified April 8, 1913.

Note: Article I, section 3, of the Constitution was modified by the 17th Amendment.

The Senate of the United States shall be composed of two Senators from each State, elected by the people thereof, for six years; and each Senator shall have one vote. The electors in each State shall have the qualifications requisite for electors of the most numerous branch of the State legislatures.

When vacancies happen in the representation of any State in the Senate, the executive authority of such State shall issue writs of election to fill such vacancies: *Provided*, That the legislature of any State may empower the executive thereof to make temporary appointments until the people fill the vacancies by election as the legislature may direct.

This amendment shall not be so construed as to affect the election or term of any Senator chosen before it becomes valid as part of the Constitution.

AMENDMENT XVIII

Passed by Congress December 18, 1917. Ratified January 16, 1919. Repealed by Amendment 21.

Section 1.

After one year from the ratification of this article the manufacture, sale, or transportation of intoxicating liquors within, the importation thereof into, or the exportation thereof from the United States and all territory subject to the jurisdiction thereof for beverage purposes is hereby prohibited.

Section 2.

The Congress and the several States shall have concurrent power to enforce this article by appropriate legislation.

Section 3.

This article shall be inoperative unless it shall have been ratified as an amendment to the Constitution by the legislatures of the several States, as provided in the Constitution, within seven years from the date of the submission hereof to the States by the Congress.

AMENDMENT XIX

Passed by Congress June 4, 1919. Ratified August 18, 1920.

The right of citizens of the United States to vote shall not be denied or abridged by the United States or by any State on account of sex.

Congress shall have power to enforce this article by appropriate legislation.

AMENDMENT XX

Passed by Congress March 2, 1932. Ratified January 23, 1933.

Note: Article I, section 4, of the Constitution was modified by section 2 of this Amendment. In addition, a portion of the 12th Amendment was superseded by section 3.

Section 1.

The terms of the President and the Vice President shall end at noon on the 20th day of January, and the terms of Senators and Representatives at noon on the 3d day of January, of the years in which such terms would have ended if this article had not been ratified; and the terms of their successors shall then begin.

Section 2.

The Congress shall assemble at least once in every year, and such meeting shall begin at noon on the 3d day of January, unless they shall by law appoint a different day.

Section 3.

If, at the time fixed for the beginning of the term of the President, the President elect shall have died, the Vice President elect shall become President. If a President shall not have been chosen before the time fixed for the beginning of his term, or if the President elect shall have failed to qualify, then the Vice President elect shall act as President until a President shall have qualified; and the Congress may by law provide for the case wherein neither a President elect nor a Vice President elect shall have qualified, declaring who shall then act as President, or the manner in which one who is to act shall be selected, and such person shall act accordingly until a President or Vice President shall have qualified.

Section 4.

The Congress may by law provide for the case of the death of any of the persons from whom the House of Representatives may choose a President whenever the right of choice shall have devolved upon them, and for the case of the death of any of the persons from whom the Senate may choose a Vice President whenever the right of choice shall have devolved upon them.

Section 5.

Sections 1 and 2 shall take effect on the 15th day of October following the ratification of this article.

Section 6.

This article shall be inoperative unless it shall have been ratified as an amendment to the Constitution by the legislatures of three-fourths of the several States within seven years from the date of its submission.

AMENDMENT XXI

Passed by Congress February 20, 1933. Ratified December 5, 1933.

Section 1.

The eighteenth article of amendment to the Constitution of the United States is hereby repealed.

Section 2.

The transportation or importation into any State, Territory, or possession of the United States for delivery or use therein of intoxicating liquors, in violation of the laws thereof, is hereby prohibited.

Section 3.

This article shall be inoperative unless it shall have been ratified as an amendment to the Constitution by conventions in the several States, as provided in the Constitution, within seven years from the date of the submission hereof to the States by the Congress.

AMENDMENT XXII

Passed by Congress March 21, 1947. Ratified February 27, 1951.

Section 1.

No person shall be elected to the office of the President more than twice, and no person who has held the office of President, or acted as President, for more than two years of a term to which some other person was elected President shall be elected to the office of the President more than once. But this Article shall not apply to any person holding the office of President when this Article was proposed by the Congress, and shall not prevent any person who may be holding the office of President, or acting as President, during the term within which this Article becomes operative from holding the office of President or acting as President during the remainder of such term.

Section 2.

This article shall be inoperative unless it shall have been ratified as an amendment to the Constitution by the legislatures of three-fourths of the several States within seven years from the date of its submission to the States by the Congress.

AMENDMENT XXIII

Passed by Congress June 16, 1960. Ratified March 29, 1961.

Section 1.

The District constituting the seat of Government of the United States shall appoint in such manner as the Congress may direct:

A number of electors of President and Vice President equal to the whole number of Senators and Representatives in Congress to which the District would be entitled if it were a State, but in no event more than the least populous State; they shall be in addition to those appointed by the States, but they shall be considered, for the purposes of the election of President and Vice President, to be electors appointed by a State; and they shall meet in the District and perform such duties as provided by the twelfth article of amendment.

Section 2.

The Congress shall have power to enforce this article by appropriate legislation.

AMENDMENT XXIV

Passed by Congress August 27, 1962. Ratified January 23, 1964.

Section 1.

The right of citizens of the United States to vote in any primary or other election for President or Vice President, for electors for President or Vice President, or for Senator or Representative in Congress, shall not be denied or abridged by the United States or any State by reason of failure to pay any poll tax or other tax.

Section 2.
The Congress shall have power to enforce this article by appropriate legislation.

AMENDMENT XXV

Passed by Congress July 6, 1965. Ratified February 10, 1967.

Note: Article II, section 1, of the Constitution was affected by the 25th amendment.

Section 1.
In case of the removal of the President from office or of his death or resignation, the Vice President shall become President.

Section 2.
Whenever there is a vacancy in the office of the Vice President, the President shall nominate a Vice President who shall take office upon confirmation by a majority vote of both Houses of Congress.

Section 3.
Whenever the President transmits to the President pro tempore of the Senate and the Speaker of the House of Representatives his written declaration that he is unable to discharge the powers and duties of his office, and until he transmits to them a written declaration to the contrary, such powers and duties shall be discharged by the Vice President as Acting President.

Section 4.
Whenever the Vice President and a majority of either the principal officers of the executive departments or of such other body as Congress may by law provide, transmit to the President pro tempore of the Senate and the Speaker of the House of Representatives their written declaration that the President is unable to discharge the powers and duties of his office, the Vice President shall immediately assume the powers and duties of the office as Acting President.

Thereafter, when the President transmits to the President pro tempore of the Senate and the Speaker of the House of Representatives his written declaration that no inability exists, he shall resume the powers and duties of his office unless the Vice President and a majority of either the principal officers of the executive department or of such other body as Congress may by law provide, transmit within four days to the President pro tempore of the Senate and the Speaker of the House of Representatives their written declaration that the President is unable to discharge the powers and duties of his office. Thereupon Congress shall decide the issue, assembling within forty-eight hours for that purpose if not in session. If the Congress, within twenty-one days after receipt of the latter written declaration, or, if Congress is not in session, within twenty-one days after Congress is required to assemble, determines by two-thirds vote of both Houses that the President is unable to discharge the powers and duties of his office, the Vice President shall continue to discharge the same as Acting President; otherwise, the President shall resume the powers and duties of his office.

AMENDMENT XXVI

Passed by Congress March 23, 1971. Ratified July 1, 1971.

Note: Amendment 14, section 2, of the Constitution was modified by section 1 of the 26th amendment.

Section 1.
The right of citizens of the United States, who are eighteen years of age or older, to vote shall not be denied or abridged by the United States or by any State on account of age.

Section 2.
The Congress shall have power to enforce this article by appropriate legislation.

AMENDMENT XXVII

Originally proposed Sept. 25, 1789. Ratified May 7, 1992.

No law, varying the compensation for the services of the Senators and Representatives, shall take effect, until an election of Representatives shall have intervened

States' Rights Under the U.S. Constitution

Selective incorporation under the 14th Amendment

The U.S. Constitution has Articles and Amendments that established constitutional rights.

The provisions in the Bill of Rights (i.e., the first ten Amendments to the Constitution) were initially binding upon only the federal government.

In time, most of these provisions became binding upon the states through *selective incorporation* into the *due process clause* of the 14th Amendment (i.e., reverse incorporation).

When a provision is made binding on a state, a state can no longer restrict the rights guaranteed in that provision.

The 1st Amendment guarantees the freedoms of speech, press, religion, and assembly.

The 5th Amendment protects the right to grand jury proceedings in federal criminal cases.

The 6th Amendment guarantees a right to confront witnesses (i.e., Confrontation Clause).

The right to confront witnesses was not *selectively incorporated* into the due process clause of the 14th Amendment and is not binding upon the states.

Therefore, persons involved in state criminal proceedings as a defendant have no federal constitutional right to grand jury proceedings.

Whether an individual has a right to a grand jury becomes a question of state law.

The 10th Amendment, which is part of the Bill of Rights, was ratified on December 15, 1791. It states the Constitution's principle of federalism by providing that powers not granted to the federal government by the Constitution, nor prohibited to the States, are reserved to the States or the people.

Federalism in the United States

Federalism in the United States is the evolving relationship between state governments and the federal government.

The American government has evolved from a system of dual federalism to associative federalism.

In "Federalist No. 46," James Madison wrote that the states and national government "are in fact but different agents and trustees of the people, constituted with different powers."

Alexander Hamilton, in "Federalist No. 28," suggested that both levels of government would exercise authority to the citizens' benefit: "If their [the peoples'] rights are invaded by either, they can make use of the other as the instrument of redress."[3]

Because the states were preexisting political entities, the U.S. Constitution did not need to define or explain federalism in one section, but it often mentions the rights and responsibilities of state governments and state officials in relation to the federal government.

The federal government has certain *express powers* (also called *enumerated powers*), which are powers spelled out in the Constitution, including the right to levy taxes, declare war, and regulate interstate and foreign commerce.

Also, the *Necessary and Proper Clause* gives the federal government the *implied power* to pass any law "necessary and proper" to execute its express powers.

Enumerated powers of the Federal Government are contained in Article I, Section 8 of the U.S. Constitution.

Other powers—the *reserved powers*—are reserved to the people or the states under the 10th Amendment. The Supreme Court decision significantly expanded the power delegated to the federal government in *McCulloch v. Maryland* (1819) and the 13th, 14th and 15th, Amendments to the Constitution following the **Civil War**.

Law Essentials series

Constitutional Law	Criminal Law and Criminal Procedure
Contracts	Business Associations
Evidence	Conflict of Laws
Real Property	Family Law
Torts	Secured Transactions
Civil Procedure	Trusts and Estates

Visit our Amazon store

Comprehensive Glossary of Legal Terms

Over 2,100 essential legal terms defined and explained. An excellent reference source for law students, practitioners and readers seeking an understanding of legal vocabulary and its application.

Landmark U.S. Supreme Court Cases: Essential Summaries

Learn important constitutional cases that shaped American law. Understand how the evolving needs of society intersect with the U.S. Constitution. Short summaries of seminal Supreme Court cases focused on issues and holdings.

Visit our Amazon store

Frank J. Addivinola, Ph.D., J.D., L.LM., MBA

The lead author and chief editor of this preparation guide is Dr. Frank Addivinola. With his outstanding education, professional training, legal and business experience, and university teaching, Dr. Addivinola lent his expertise to develop this book.

Attorney Frank Addivinola is admitted to practice law in several jurisdictions. He has served as an academic advisor and mentor for students and practitioners.

Dr. Addivinola holds an undergraduate degree from Williams College. He completed his Masters at Harvard University, Masters in Biotechnology at Johns Hopkins University, Masters in Technology Management and MBA at the University of Maryland University College, J.D. and L.LM. from Suffolk University, and Ph.D. in Law and Public Policy from Northeastern University.

During his extensive teaching career, Dr. Addivinola taught university courses in Introduction to Law and developed law coursebooks. He received several awards for community service, research, and presentations.

www.ingramcontent.com/pod-product-compliance
Lightning Source LLC
Chambersburg PA
CBHW081345070526
44578CB00005B/729